GUINNESS WORLD RECORDS

N E Lincs Libraries

5 4073 02006408 7

KT-159-566

AMAZING ANIMALS

ACKNOWLEDGEMENTS

Senior Project Editor
Adam Millward

Editor-in-Chief
Craig Glenday

Senior Managing Editor
Stephen Fall

Project Editor
Ben Hollingum

Layout Editors
Sophie Barling,
Alice Peebles

Gaming Editor
Stephen Daultrey

Information & Research Manager
Carim Valerio

VP Publishing
Jenny Heller

Head of Pictures & Design
Michael Whitty

Picture Editor
Fran Morales

Picture Researcher
Saffron Fradley

Talent Researchers
Jenny Langridge,
Victoria Tweedy

Designer
Billy Waqar

Assistant Designer
Gareth Butterworth

Original Illustrations
Tripp Yeoman

Production Director
Patricia Magill

Publishing Manager
Jane Boatfield

Production Assistant
Thomas McCurdy

Production Consultants
Roger Hawkins, Dennis Thon,
Tobias Wrona

Reprographics
Res Kahraman at Born Group

Printing & Binding
MOHN Media Mohndruck GmbH,
Gütersloh, Germany

Original Photography
Jonathan Browning,
James Cannon,
Paul Michael Hughes,
Kevin Scott Ramos,
Ryan Schude

Indexer
Marie Lorimer

Consultant
Dr Karl P N Shuker

Proofreading
Matthew White

British Library Cataloguing-in-publication data: a catalogue record for this book is available from the British Library

UK: 978-1-910561-61-4
US: 978-1-910561-62-1
US: 978-1-910561-90-4

Records are made to be broken – indeed, it is one of the key criteria for a record category – so if you find a record that you think you can beat, tell us about it by making a record claim. Always contact us before making a record attempt.

Check **www.guinnessworldrecords.com** regularly for record-breaking news, plus video footage of record attempts. You can also join and interact with the Guinness World Records online community.

Sustainability
The paper used for this edition is manufactured by UPM Plattling, Germany. The production site has forest certification and its operations have both ISO14001 environmental management system and EMAS certification to ensure sustainable production.

UPM Papers are true Biofore products, produced from renewable and recyclable materials.

Guinness World Records Limited has a very thorough accreditation system for records verification. However, while every effort is made to ensure accuracy, Guinness World Records Limited cannot be held responsible for any errors contained in this work. Feedback from our readers on any point of accuracy is always welcomed.

Guinness World Records Limited uses both metric and imperial measurements. The sole exceptions are for some scientific data where metric measurements only are universally accepted, and for some sports data. Where a specific date is given, the exchange rate is calculated according to the currency values that were in operation at the time. Where only a year date is given, the exchange rate is calculated from 31 Dec of that year. "One billion" is taken to mean one thousand million.

Appropriate advice should always be taken when attempting to break or set records. Participants undertake records entirely at their own risk. Guinness World Records Limited has complete discretion over whether or not to include any particular record attempts in any of its publications. Being a Guinness World Records record holder does not guarantee you a place in any Guinness World Records publication.

OFFICIALLY AMAZING

THE JIM PATTISON GROUP

CORPORATE OFFICE
Global President: Alistair Richards

Professional Services
Chief Financial Officer: Alison Ozanne
Financial Controller: Andrew Wood
Accounts Receivable Manager: Lisa Gibbs
Finance Managers:
Jaimie-Lee Emrith, Daniel Ralph
Assistant Accountants: Jess Blake, Yusuf Gafar
Accounts Payable Clerk: Tajkiya Sultana
Accounts Receivable Clerk:
Jusna Begum
Trading Analysis Manager:
Elizabeth Bishop
General Counsel: Raymond Marshall
Legal Counsel: Terence Tsang
Junior Legal Counsel: Xiangyun Rablen
Paralegal: Michelle Phua
Global HR Director: Farrella Ryan-Coker
HR Assistant: Mehreen Saeed
Office Manager: Jackie Angus
Director of IT: Rob Howe
IT Manager: James Edwards
Developers: Cenk Selim, Lewis Ayers
Desktop Administrator: Alpha Serrant-Defoe
Analyst / Tester: Céline Bacon
Global SVP Records: Marco Frigatti
Head of Category Management:
Jacqueline Sherlock
Information & Research Manager:
Carim Valerio
RMT Training Manager: Alexandra Popistan
Category Managers: Adam Brown, Tripp Yeoman, Victoria Tweedy
Category Executive: Danielle Kirby
Records Consultant: Sam Mason

Global Brand Strategy
SVP Global Brand Strategy:
Samantha Fay
Brand Manager: Juliet Dawson
VP Creative: Paul O'Neill
Head of Global Production Delivery:
Alan Pixsley

Global Product Marketing
VP Global Product Marketing:
Katie Forde
Director of Global TV Content & Sales:
Rob Molloy
Senior TV Distribution Manager:
Paul Glynn
Senior TV Content Executive
& Production Co-ordinator:
Jonathan Whitton
Head of Digital: Veronica Irons
Online Editor: Kevin Lynch
Online Writer: Rachel Swatman
Social Media Manager: Dan Thorne
Digital Video Producer: Matt Musson
Junior Video Producer: Cécile Thai
Front-End Developer: Alex Waldu
Brand & Consumer Product Marketing Manager: Lucy Acfield
B2B Product Marketing Manager (Live Events): Louise Toms
B2B Product Marketing Manager (PR & Advertising): Emily Osborn
Product Marketing Executive: Victor Fenes
Designer: Rebecca Buchanan Smith
Junior Designer: Edward Dillon

EMEA & APAC
SVP EMEA APAC: Nadine Causey
Head of Publishing Sales: John Pilley
Key Accounts Manager: Caroline Lake
Publishing Rights and Export Manager:
Helene Navarre
Distribution Executive: Alice Oluyitan
Head of Commercial Accounts & Licensing:
Sam Prosser
Business Development Managers:
Lee Harrison, Alan Southgate
Commercial Account Managers: Jessica Rae, Inga Rasmussen, Sadie Smith, Fay Edwards
Country Representative – Business Development Manager, India: Nikhil Shukla
PR Director: Jakki Lewis
Senior PR Manager: Doug Male
B2B PR Manager: Melanie DeFries
International Press Officer:
Amber-Georgina Gill
Head of Marketing:
Justine Tommey / Chriscilla Philogene
Senior B2B Marketing Manager:
Mawa Rodriguez
B2C Marketing Manager: Christelle Betrong
Content Marketing Executive: Imelda Ekpo
Head of Records Management, APAC:
Ben Backhouse
Head of Records Management, Europe:
Shantha Chinniah
Records Managers: Mark McKinley,
Christopher Lynch, Matilda Hagne, Daniel Kidane, Sheila Mella
Records Executive: Megan Double
Senior Production Manager:
Fiona Gruchy-Craven
Project Manager: Cameron Kellow
Country Manager, MENA: Talal Omar
Head of RMT, MENA: Samer Khallouf
Records Manager, MENA: Hoda Khachab
B2B Marketing Manager, MENA: Leila Issa
Commercial Account Managers, MENA:
Khalid Yassine, Kamel Yassin
Official Adjudicators:
Ahmed Gamal Gabr, Anna Orford, Brian Sobel, Glenn Pollard, Jack Brockbank, Lena Kuhlmann, Lorenzo Veltri, Lucia Sinigagliesi, Paulina Sapinska, Pete Fairbairn, Pravin Patel, Richard Stenning, Kevin Southam, Rishi Nath, Seyda Subasi-Gemici, Sofia Greenacre, Solvej Malouf, Swapnil Dangarikar

AMERICAS
SVP Americas: Peter Harper
VP Marketing & Commercial Sales:
Keith Green
VP Publishing Sales, Americas:
Walter Weintz
Director of Latin America:
Carlos Martinez
Head of Brand Development, West Coast:
Kimberly Partrick
Head of Commercial Sales: Nicole Pando
Senior Account Manager: Ralph Hannah
Account Managers: Alex Angert, Giovanni Bruna, Mackenzie Berry
Project Manager: Casey DeSantis
PR Manager: Kristen Ott
Assistant PR Manager: Elizabeth Montoya
PR Coordinator: Sofia Rocher
Digital Coordinator: Kristen Stephenson
Publishing Sales Manager: Lisa Corrado

Marketing Manager: Morgan Kubelka
Consumer Marketing Executive:
Tavia Levy
Senior Records Manager, North America:
Hannah Ortman
Senior Records Manager, Latin America:
Raquel Assis
Records Managers, North America:
Michael Furnari, Kaitlin Holl, Kaitlin Vesper
Records Manager, Latin America:
Sarah Casson
HR & Office Manager: Kellie Ferrick
Official Adjudicators, North America:
Michael Empric, Philip Robertson,
Christina Flounders Conlon, Jimmy Coggins,
Andrew Glass, Mike Janela
Official Adjudicators, Latin America:
Natalia Ramirez Talero, Carlos Tapia Rojas

JAPAN
VP Japan: Erika Ogawa
Office Manager: Fumiko Kitagawa
Director of RMT: Kaoru Ishikawa
Records Managers: Mariko Koike,
Yoko Furuya
Records Executive: Koma Satoh
Marketing Director: Hideki Naruse
Designer: Momoko Cunneen
Senior PR & Sales Promotion Manager:
Kazami Kamioka
B2B Marketing Manager PR & Advertising:
Asumi Funatsu
Project Manager Live Events: Aya McMillan
Digital & Publishing Content Manager:
Takafumi Suzuki
Commercial Director: Vihag Kulshrestha
Account Managers:
Takuro Maruyama, Masamichi Yazaki
Senior Account Executive:
Daisuke Katayama
Account Executive: Minami Ito
Official Adjudicators: Justin Patterson,
Mai McMillan, Gulnaz Ukassova, Rei Iwashita

GREATER CHINA
President: Rowan Simons
General Manager, Greater China:
Marco Frigatti
VP Commercial, Global & Greater China:
Blythe Fitzwiliam
Senior Account Manager:
Catherine Gao
Senior Project Manager: Reggy Lu
Account Manager: Chloe Liu
External Relations Manager:
Dong Cheng
Digital Business Manager: Jacky Yuan
Head of RMT: Charles Wharton
Records Manager: Alicia Zhao
Records Manager / Project Co-ordinator:
Fay Jiang
HR & Office Manager: Tina Shi
Office Assistant: Kate Wang
Head of Marketing: Wendy Wang
B2B Marketing Manager: Iris Hou
Digital Manager: Lily Zeng
Marketing Executive: Tracy Cui
PR Manager: Ada Liu
Content Director: Angela Wu
Official Adjudicators: Brittany Dunn,
Joanne Brent, John Garland, Maggie Luo,
Peter Yang

© 2017 GUINNESS WORLD RECORDS LIMITED
No part of this book may be reproduced or transmitted in any form or by any means, electronic, chemical, mechanical, including photography, or used in any information storage or retrieval system without a licence or other permission in writing from the copyright owners.

WELCOME...

HEY, EVERYONE!

It's me – Jiffpom! It's a privilege to introduce you to the very first edition of *Guinness World Records: Amazing Animals*. If you love cute critters and talented pets – and who could blame you? – then you're in for a real treat.

I'm delighted that we animals are finally getting our very own *Guinness World Records* book. Don't get me wrong, human record-breakers are fantastic too, but everyone knows that four legs are better than two, right?

Even I was shocked by the sheer variety of furry feats being achieved by dogs, cats (obviously not quite as good as those by dogs), rabbits, monkeys, lizards – and just about every other creature you can think of. Setting records isn't easy – and that's speaking from experience.

I earned my first two GWR titles by walking on two legs. It's a trick I had to perfect for my cameo in Katy Perry's music video "Dark Horse" – YouTube it!

Now I have a brand-new achievement to celebrate... Thanks to all my online fans, I'm the **most followed dog on Instagram**, with almost 5 million followers! Find out what I've been up to lately on my page: @jiffpom. If you can't wait, head to pp.84–85 for a whole feature about me in the Celebrity Animals chapter.

I'm a firm believer that every animal has got a record in them. It's just about finding the thing that you can do better than the next Pomeranian. As you enjoy this book with your humans, just think: what could be *my* record? Who knows, perhaps you'll be in the next edition!

Jiffpom

Jiffpom poses with his GWR certificate as the **most followed dog on Instagram**.

CERTIFICATE

Jiffpom (USA) is the most popular dog on Instagram, with 4.6 million followers as of 19 April 2017

OFFICIALLY AMAZING

CONTENTS

ANIMAL WONDERS

WILD THINGS

ON THE MOVE

ANIMAL RESCUES

CELEBRITY ANIMALS

AMAZING ANIMALS

Welcome to the very first *Guinness World Records: Amazing Animals* – a brand-new book dedicated to record-breaking creatures from all around the world! From unbelievable pet tricks and superlative zoos to the critters that everyone's following on social media, there really is something for every kind of animal-lover. Keep an eye out for our special superhero-themed features (right) and all sorts of wild activities (see opposite).

GUINNESS WORLD RECORDS

AMAZING ANIMALS

PACKED FULL OF YOUR MOST-LOVED ANIMAL FRIENDS

TEST YOUR SUPERPET'S IQ

Galleries compare animals with something in common

Bite-sized pieces of wildlife trivia

What animals are really thinking...

Jokes to get your friends laughing like hyenas!

Stunning wildlife photography

Put your nature knowledge to the test

"100%" symbols indicate an animal is shown life-size

SUPER SNOUTS

FURRY FASHIONISTAS

BIG PICTURE

HAIRY HEROES!

THE CHIMERA!
LOL
QUICK QUIZ

EPIC JOURNEYS

FUN & GAMES

Inside *Amazing Animals*, you'll find loads of original games and activities to sink your teeth into! Design your very own record-breaking beast with our online animal builder, test out your pet's IQ and make an origami frog – plus much more!

DOG IQ TEST
FUR-THER INFO
FAST FACT

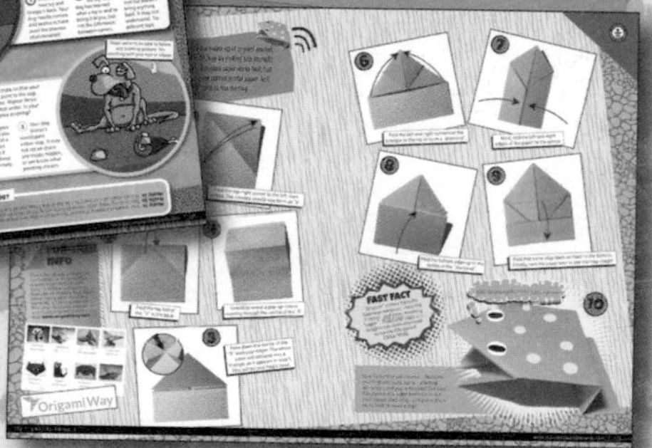
FAST FACT
Origami Way

Sidebars offer related records and trivia

Cool facts about a particular animal family

NDA-MONIUM!
FACTS AT YOUR FINGERTIPS
NO WAY! Pandas were not heard of in the West until 1869!
DATA FILE

Species-specific key statistics

IS *MY* PET A RECORD-BREAKER?

Official GWR adjudicator Victoria Tweedy (pictured below with the tallest dog, Freddy; see pp.190–91) answers a few FAQs about animal record-breaking.

Are there any pets that *can't* get a record?
In general, all pets have to be deemed domesticated, fully grown and signed off as healthy. That means that healthy adult cats, dogs, rabbits, guinea pigs and sheep are fine, but young animals, ill pets or wild animals, such as tigers, would not be allowed.

Do you have any records for pet tricks?
We do! With all of our trick categories, the animals can't be touched during the attempt so we know that they're doing the activity voluntarily. It's important to us that animals are happy to take part.

Can pets and owners set records together?
We have a number of records involving team activities, such as **most skips by a human and dog in a minute**. Of course, even records that involve just the pet need lots of training input and encouragement from the owner.

Do you have records for heaviest pets?
We don't monitor records for pets based on weight. While your dog or cat might be naturally big, we wouldn't want any pet being overfed just to achieve a record.

How do I prove that my pet has set a record?
Sometimes, an adjudicator like me witnesses an attempt live or measures a potential record in person. Alternatively, you can send us evidence and our team of experts will review it. To apply to break an existing title or to suggest a new category, visit **www.guinnessworldrecords.com**. Good luck!

BLEACH BOYS

Think "tiger", and you think black stripes on orange, right? Very occasionally, however, these majestic moggies come out... white. The amazing colourless cats are extremely rare in the wild: for one of these tigers to be born, both parents must carry the gene for white colouring (caused by a lack of the pigment "pheomelanin"). That only happens naturally about once in 10,000 tiger births! Seek out pp.14–15 to discover more of the animal kingdom's white wonders...

ANIMAL WONDERS

TOP 10

LARGEST LITTER OF...

If good things come in small packages, we're spoiling you many times over with these bundles of joy! Coo over these records for the most mammals born at the same time...

1 PIGS

The average litter size for a domestic pig is 12. Back in 1993, however, a sow (female pig) on a farm in York, UK, "farrowed" 37 piglets! The mother was a cross between a Large White Duroc and a Meishan pig, a Chinese breed known for large litters. Of the 36 piglets born alive, 33 survived, which is an amazing result. Piglets are more likely to thrive if the sow builds a decent "nest".

2 MICE

In 1982, a mouse belonging to M Ogilvie of Blackpool, UK, gave birth to 34 baby mice ("pups"), 33 of which survived. The average litter size is nine, but females can produce up to 10 litters per year!

3 TENRECS

The average litter for a tailless tenrec is already sizeable at 15, but the largest known is 31! That gives the hedgehog-like insectivore from Madagascar the record for **largest litter for a wild mammal**.

4 HAMSTERS

In 1974, a hamster belonging to the Miller family of Louisiana, USA, gave birth to 26 hamsters. The average is eight offspring per litter.

Tenrecs share a common ancestry with aardvarks, elephants and manatees.

7 CATS

Considering that the average litter for a domestic cat is five, 19 kittens is a feline feat! The furry bundles were born in 1970 to a Burmese-Siamese cross belonging to V Gane of Kingham, UK.

=5 DOGS

The **largest litter of dogs** on record is 24, born in 2004 to Tia, a Neapolitan mastiff. She was owned by Damian Ward and Anne Kellegher from Cambridgeshire, UK. The average number of puppies in a single birth is eight, though this number varies widely depending on the breed.

=5 RABBITS

In 1978, a New Zealand rabbit gave birth to 24 babies (aka "kits"). The typical litter size is just six, but rabbits are notoriously fast breeders. Owing to their short pregnancies female rabbits can have litters as often as one every month!

9 TEST-TUBE DOGS

Scientists can now help breed puppies using a technique called "IVF" (in-vitro fertilization). It's hoped this will help us protect rare breeds at risk of disappearing. In 2015, US scientists from Cornell University and the Smithsonian Institution used this process to conceive seven pups – the **first litter of test-tube dogs**.

8 GUINEA PIGS

The average litter size for a guinea pig is four. However, a guinea pig named Casperina from Australia bucked the trend. She gave birth to a staggering nine "pups" in 1992!

10 BEARS

Bears usually have very small litters, with an average of two cubs. The most born at once in captivity, however, is five. Three male and two female brown bears were welcomed to Košice Zoo in Slovakia in 2002. They were named Miso, Tapik, Dazzle, Bubu and Cindy.

FAST FACT
The seven test-tube dogs had two different fathers (a cocker spaniel and a beagle) and three different beagle mothers. This resulted in five pure beagle puppies and two beagle-cocker-spaniel crosses.

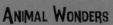

HYBRIDS

What do you get when you cross...? You may know a joke or two that starts like this. But joking aside, cross-species creatures are very much a reality. The animals that result from these mixed-parent pairings are known as hybrids.

NO WAY!

Hercules eats 30 lb (13.6 kg) of meat a day!

LIGER

Meet Hercules, the **largest living cat** and one of the most famous hybrids of all time. He has an African lion father and a Bengal tiger mother, but he is bigger than either of his parents! Ligers only occur in captivity, because these species would never naturally meet. Hercules measures 10 ft 11 in (3.3 m) long and weighs in at 922 lb (418.2 kg) – a little under the weight of a concert grand piano! He lives at the Myrtle Beach Safari reserve – aka T.I.G.E.R.S. – in South Carolina, USA.

WHITE LIGER

Hercules could soon be facing competition for his title – from his own relatives, no less! In 2014, Myrtle Beach Safari welcomed four new additions: Yeti, Odin, Sampson and Apollo. The cubs – who are Hercules' nephews – were the offspring of white lion Ivory and white tiger Saraswati (below). The furry foursome were the **first white ligers**. The reserve's director believes that Yeti – the largest of the litter – is most likely to outgrow his uncle.

There are only around 300 white lions in captivity worldwide.

PUMAPARD

In the late 1800s, a private zoo in Germany successfully bred a brand-new cross-species of cat. The half-puma, half-leopard felines became known as "pumapards" (when the father was a puma) and "lepumas" (when the father was a leopard). They were the **first big cat/small cat hybrids** ever born.

ZONKEY

Mix a zebra with another member of the horse family and you get a "zebroid". These include "zorses" (zebra-horses) and "zonies" (zebra-ponies). It was once believed that zebras and donkeys were biologically incompatible. However, "zonkeys" such as this stripy foal have been born at zoos and on rare occasions have been spotted in the wild.

SAVANNAH CAT

This mega-moggy was called "Savannah Islands Trouble". At 19 in (48.3 cm) from shoulder to toe, he was once the **tallest domestic cat** (check out the current holder on pp.188–89). Savannah cats such as "Trouble" are so big because they are part serval – a type of wild cat that lives in Africa.

check out the current holder on pp.188–89

CAMA

Born in 1998 at a research centre in Dubai, UAE, Rama was the **first camel-llama hybrid**. His parents would never have met in the wild, as they live on different continents, but they both belong to the camel family. Dad was a dromedary camel and Mum was a llama.

LOL

WHAT DO YOU GET WHEN YOU CROSS A FISH WITH AN ELEPHANT?

SWIMMING TRUNKS!

HYBRID ANIMAL QUIZ

Can you guess the names of the offspring that result from these cross-species pairings? Find the answers on pp.210–11.

Find the answers on pp.210–11.

+

+

+

WHITE WONDERS

Sometimes in the animal kingdom, you find creatures that stand out from their brothers and sisters because they're totally white! The causes of colour loss are varied, but it can occur in any animal, from reptiles to birds and even humans.

2

3

Little Snowflake fathered 21 gorillas – none of which were white like him.

1

4

1 This wide-eyed critter is a white slow loris from Indonesia. These primates – which normally have brown and grey-coloured fur – may look cute, but are actually toxic. They obtain venom from a gland in their elbows, which they lick to gain a deadly bite.

2 Little Snowflake – once deemed the **rarest gorilla specimen** owing to his unique colour – lived at Barcelona Zoo in Spain until his death in 2003. His blue eyes suggest he did not have true albinism but a similar disorder. He's one of the most photographed animals of all time.

3 This white wonder is actually a green turtle – a species named after the greenish fat under its skin rather than its outer appearance. The black turtles surrounding it are its naturally coloured siblings; the juveniles become lighter and more speckled as they grow up.

6

FAST FACT
Among fully coloured peacocks, only the males boast the dazzling blue and green plumage. The females are mainly brown – largely to help them stay camouflaged while raising their peachicks.

5

FUR-THER INFO

There are many reasons why some animals are born white. But essentially it's down to pigment – or a lack of it! Whether you have brown eyes or blue, blond hair or red, the colour is determined by a pigment called "melanin", produced by dedicated cells. When these cells are faulty, only certain pigments – or in the case of true albinos, no pigments – are made by the body. This albinism results in white hair, pale skin and transparent irises in the eyes, which makes them appear red.

7

4 Measuring in at 7 m (23 ft), Twinkie was the **longest albino snake in captivity ever** and one of the star residents at The Reptile Zoo in Fountain Valley, California, USA. Twinkie was a reticulated python, which is the **longest snake species**.

5 Le Cornelle Animal Park in Valbrembo, Italy, welcomed baby Pino the red-necked wallaby to their reserve in 2007. Wallabies tend to have grey and brown fur, so it came as a big surprise when pure-white Pino first popped his head out of his mother's pouch!

6 White peacocks are not albinos. In the past, some scientists believed that these stunning birds were their own species. We now know that they are, in fact, a genetic mutation of the Indian blue. Curiously, the chicks are born yellow and fade to white as they mature.

7 It's extremely rare for white tigers to occur in the wild, but one place where you're guaranteed to see them is Nandankanan Zoo. This wildlife park in the state of Odisha, India, boasts the **largest population of white tigers** in the world. As of 2015, it was home to eight.

ASTRO-ANIMALS

Meet the intrepid animals who have got closer to the stars than most earthlings! They were the first astronauts to be catapulted into the unknown, and human space missions only became possible because of them.

DOG
1,659 KM
1,030 MI

Russian Laika (which means "Barker") took off on 3 Nov 1957 in *Sputnik 2*, becoming the **first animal to orbit Earth**. The street dog from Moscow has since been honoured with a rocket-shaped statue in her home city.

BULLFROGS
574 KM
356 MI

In 1970, NASA launched its Frogs in Space (FRIS) experiment by sending two bullfrogs into orbit. Like humans, frogs have a balancing mechanism in their ears and the amphibians taught us a lot about living in space.

SPIDERS
435 KM
270 MI

Garden spiders Arabella and Anita joined the US Skylab 3 mission in 1973 to test their web-building skills in space. Their silk was finer than usual, but their designs were perfect. Result? The **first spider webs in space!**

RHESUS MONKEY & SQUIRREL MONKEY
483 KM
300 MI

Taking off from the USA on 28 May 1959, rhesus monkey Miss Able (far left) and tiny squirrel monkey Miss Baker (left) made history as the **first monkeys to survive a space flight.**

TORTOISES
380,000 KM
236,121 MI

A pair of Russian tortoises were the **first animals to circle the Moon**, in the Soviet *Zond 5* spacecraft in 1968. Their flight went into deep space and made the first lunar flyby before returning to Earth. Afterwards, scientists found the shelled astronauts had lost weight but were in good health.

WATER BEARS

305 KM 189 MI

In 2007, microscopic tardigrades – aka water bears – went into orbit for 10 days, proving to be the **hardiest animals in outer space**. After being exposed to the lack of oxygen and extreme radiation levels unassisted.

CHIMPANZEE

252 KM 157 MI

The **first ape to survive a space flight** was Ham, launched by NASA from Cape Canaveral in Florida, USA, on 31 Jan 1961. The astro-chimp operated a lever when prompted, flew for just over 16 min and made a safe landing back on Earth.

MOUSE

137 KM 85 MI

On 31 Aug 1950, the **first mouse in space** flew on a US V-2 rocket from New Mexico, USA, blazing the way for other rodent astronauts – including the **first rats in space** a decade later.

RABBIT

52 KM 31 MI

On 2 Jul 1959, plucky Marfusha ("Little Martha") made one giant hop for the animal kingdom as the **first rabbit in space**. The grey bunny was part of a menagerie of dogs, rats, mice and fruit flies all on board an R2-A rocket launched by the Soviet Union.

RHESUS MONKEY

134 KM 83 MI

Albert II took part in one of many US missions carrying a monkey crew. On 14 Jun 1949, he achieved lasting fame as the **first monkey in space**, having passed the 100-km (62-mi) boundary that marks the edge of the atmosphere.

FAST FACT

Ham the chimp (right) received training for his flight and proved that tasks could be performed in a weightless environment. His success led to the USA's first human space flight, by Alan Shepard in 1961.

Hear the word "babies" and you think of small and cuddly, right? But some offspring from the world of animals can be even bigger than grown-up humans! Their size doesn't make them any less cute, though!

BIG BABIES

GIRAFFE

The planet's **tallest mammals** arrive with a bump when born – dropping about 6 ft (1.8 m) to the ground! Once they've recovered from the tumble, they're on their feet within an hour. Baby giraffes stand taller than an average man.

DATA FILE

COMMON NAME:
Giraffe

SCIENTIFIC NAME:
Giraffa camelopardalis

TYPE: Mammal

LOCATION: Africa

HEIGHT: Adult: 5.5 m (18 ft); baby: 2 m (6 ft 6 in)

TONGUE LENGTH: 50 cm (20 in)

ELEPHANT

It won't come as any surprise that the **largest land mammal** also gives birth to the largest offspring on land. African elephant calves weigh in the region of 200 lb (90 kg), which is roughly the same as 25 human babies! Elephants also have the **longest gestation period for a mammal**, with Asian elephants carrying their babies for up to 760 days – that's more than two years!

Elephant calves gain 2-3 lb (1-1.3 kg) per day in their first year.

HIPPOPOTAMUS

Baby hippos make a big splash on entering the world, as the females give birth in water. The calves have to swim to the surface to draw their first breath, often with a gentle nudge from their mother. The babies weigh up to 50 kg (110 lb) at birth, which is about the same as an adult Rottweiler! Calves can suckle while underwater by closing their nostrils.

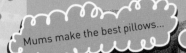

Mums make the best pillows...

NO WAY!

A baby blue whale's daily ration of milk would easily fill a bathtub!

FAST FACT

Hippos spend a lot of time underwater to keep cool. Special membranes cover their eyes, acting like a natural pair of goggles.

SIBERIAN TIGER

Tiger cubs may not be on quite the same scale as the other big babies here, but they are huge for cats. Newborns can weigh in excess of 1.6 kg (3 lb 8 oz). That's about the same weight as 16 domestic kittens! The Siberian tiger is the **largest feline carnivore** and **largest wild cat**, with adult males tipping the scales at 180–300 kg (400–660 lb).

BLUE WHALE

Imagine a newborn that weighs the same as three cows! That's how heavy a baby blue whale can be – easily making it the **largest offspring** in the animal kingdom. That's tiny compared to its parents, though. Blue whales are the **largest mammal ever** – bigger than any dinosaur. They can reach 30 m (98 ft) in length, which is as long as a Boeing 737 jumbo jet!

ROBO-ANIMALS

They jump, they slither, they fly, they swim – but they're not real animals! These robots combine the best bits of nature and technology and have set a few records along the way.

FAST FACT

Scientists used several methods to determine the health benefits of PARO. Interviews assessed changes in patients' daily routines and social interaction, while urine tests revealed a change in hormone levels indicating a reduction in stress.

The super-cute seal responds to human touch and sound.

PARO

In 2001, an adorable robo-seal called PARO was placed into a care home in Japan to see if its fluffy presence might help relax the residents. The results showed that people who had spent time engaging with the bot were noticeably more relaxed than those who hadn't. This meant PARO had *seal*ed the record for **most therapeutic robot**.

You're sure electronics and water mix, right?

SHOAL "ROBO-FISH"

An unusual shoal joined marine life in Gijón harbour, Spain, in 2012. It was made up of the **largest robotic fish**, each 1.5 m (4 ft 11 in) long. They swim like real fish and are equipped with sonar to avoid obstacles and communicate with each other. Their job is to patrol the seas to detect pollution.

TITANOBOA

You need plenty of wiggle room when you're 50 ft (15 m) long and weigh 1,750 lb (800 kg). But who wouldn't make way for Titanoboa, the **largest robot snake**? A team at the eatART lab in Vancouver, Canada, used fossil evidence to build Titanoboa, based on a real prehistoric snake. The robo-serpent, which has a hydraulic system that allows it to slither along at 2.5 mph (4 km/h), sometimes takes to the dancefloor at festivals around North America.

What's he looking at?!

Debuting in 2017, British TV series *Spy in the Wild* uses animatronic creatures fitted with cameras to get up close with wildlife. Here, "Spy Monkey" (right) was accepted into a friendly tribe of langur monkeys.

100%

ROBOBEE

Microbots inspired by bees took flight in 2013 at Harvard University in the USA. Propelled by wafer-thin wings that flap 120 times per sec, they achieved the **first controlled flight by a robotic insect**. A RoboBee, less than half the size of a paper clip, weighs only 0.002 oz (56 mg) so is also the **lightest flying robot**. They might not look like bees particularly, but it's thought that in future they could be used in large groups to pollinate crops. Busy, busy, if not buzzy!

The mechanical giraffe reveals the neck structure of the world's **tallest mammal**.

BIONICKANGAROO

A kangaroo moves in a unique way, using the energy from one leap to power itself into the next. Festo's BionicKangaroo has motors, valves and an air reservoir to help it jump just like the real thing. Controlled by hand gestures from a human operator, this *roo*-bot can leap with the best of them.

In 2017, the Horniman Museum in London, UK, played host to a "Robot Zoo". The special exhibition featured outsized robotic beasts to explain the inner workings of the real-life animals. Among its stars were a giraffe (above), a fly, a chameleon and a giant squid.

CAT ISLAND

Aoshima in Ehime Prefecture, Japan, is the *purr*-fect destination for cat-lovers. The little island – only one mile (1.6 km) long – is home to just a handful of people but an entire colony of cats!

As soon as visitors step off the ferry, they're greeted by a whiskered welcoming party. The cats often patrol Aoshima's harbour, on the off-chance of receiving a free lunch. Most of the cats are semi-tame and know exactly how to catch the attention of tourists – many of whom venture to this island solely to see them.

So why are there so many cats on Aoshima? A few felines were originally introduced to hunt mice on the islanders' fishing boats. However, many of the pets became feral as more and more residents left the island (there were 900 people in 1945 and only about 20 today). With fewer owners to keep the cat community in check, the population was left to its own devices and boomed.

NO WAY!

Cats outnumber people by 6 to 1 on Aoshima!

The public are discouraged from feeding the cats. But there are set areas where islanders do offer food. One of the few people to live on Aoshima is Atsuko Ogata, the village nurse. Here, she dishes out biscuits to a hungry horde at one of the designated "feeding stations", while above she gives one cat a check-up.

Aoshima is the most famous "cat island", but it's not unique. In fact, there are more than 10 dotted around Japanese waters, including Enoshima in Kanagawa Prefecture and Genkaishima in Fukuoka Prefecture. They are all former fishing colonies that have declined, leaving the moggy populations to soar!

OTHER ANIMAL ISLANDS

Christmas Island: Once a year, around 50 million red crabs on Australia's Christmas Island embark on a mass migration from the forest to the shore to breed. They travel in regimented columns, generally following the same routes annually.

Pig Island: The uninhabited isle of Big Major Cay in The Bahamas is famed for its beach-dwelling pigs. The feral swine love nothing more than to take a dip to cool down in the Caribbean heat.

Rabbit Island: If cats aren't for you, Japan also offers Okunoshima in Hiroshima Prefecture. Although no one's certain how the bunnies first arrived, the current population is in the hundreds. They are now one of the island's biggest attractions.

FARMYARD GIANTS

Some farmyard friends have made a *big* impression on their owners, as well as in the world of records. If Old MacDonald had owned all of this large livestock, he would definitely have needed a bigger farm!

FACTS
at your FINGERTIPS

You may have heard that a cow has four stomachs. In fact, they only have one stomach, divided into four parts.

A cow chews about 50 times a minute and moves its jaws some 40,000 times a day.

Cows have almost 360-degree vision and can detect smells up to 6 mi (9.6 km) away.

BIG JAKE

The **tallest living horse** is Big Jake, a Belgian standing 210.1 cm (6 ft 10.7 in) tall. He was measured, without shoes, at Smokey Hollow Farms in Poynette, Wisconsin, USA, on 19 Jan 2010. He is now enjoying a well-earned retirement.

95.2 cm (3 ft 1 in)

LURCH

The **largest horn circumference on a steer ever** measured 95.2 cm (3 ft 1 in) in 2003. The proud holder was Lurch (right), an African watusi steer owned by Janice Wolf of Gassville in Arkansas, USA. Two vets measured three times to confirm the incredible circumference. Lurch's horns spanned an impressive 210 cm (6 ft 10 in), but that's not a patch on the **longest horns for a steer ever**. That honour goes to Gibraltar (inset), a Texas longhorn with a combined horn length of 10 ft 4.7 in (316 cm).

10 ft 4.7 in (316 cm)

NO WAY!

Blosom could poop up to 8 ft (2.4 m) away!

BLOSOM

Gentle giant Blosom (left) was the **tallest cow ever**, standing 190 cm (6 ft 2 in) from hoof to withers on 24 May 2014. A stepladder was needed to help measure her! Blosom was born to two average-sized parents of the Holstein breed. Patty Meads-Hanson (pictured) of Orangeville in Illinois, USA, met her when she was eight weeks old and treated her like a pet. She said Blosom loved having her chin rubbed and ears scratched.

ROMULUS

The **tallest living donkey** is Romulus, an American Mammoth Jackstock, who stood 172.7 cm (5 ft 8 in) tall on 8 Feb 2013. Romulus is owned by Cara and Phil Yellott of Red Oak in Texas, USA. Romulus's brother and companion Remus is almost as huge, so it must be in the genes! By comparison, most members of this breed stand under 150 cm (4 ft 11 in) tall.

The Mammoth Jackstock was first bred by US President George Washington (1732–99).

ANIMAL WONDERS

BIG PICTURE

KING OF THE CRABS

To say that coconut crabs are a little bigger than your average crab would be an understatement. They are, in fact, the world's **heaviest land crustacean**, with the largest specimens tipping the scales at 4.1 kg (9 lb) and spanning 1 m (39 in). Even average-sized members of this species are a hefty 2.5 kg (5 lb 8 oz), with a leg-span of 91 cm (36 in).

Native to tropical islands in the Indian and Pacific Oceans, they feed mainly on decomposing coconuts that have fallen off palm trees. However, they are also opportunistic scavengers, often raiding human garbage (see left) – hence their nickname of "robber crabs".

To put the size of coconut crabs into context, the biggest one ever recorded weighed roughly the same as 205 Roborovski hamsters – the **smallest hamster species.**

THE CHIMERA!

A chimera – pronounced "kai-MEE-ra" – is a creature from Greek mythology. It's a fusion of a lion, a goat and a snake. In tribute to this mythological monster, we've created our very own version of a chimera, not with three animals but seven! The one thing that all these curious critters have in common is that they – or at least parts of them – are record holders. Can you work out each species in this hilarious hybrid? The answers are on the next page.

LOL

WHAT DO YOU GET WHEN YOU CROSS A PARROT WITH A CENTIPEDE?

A WALKIE-TALKIE!

MAKE YOUR OWN! Feeling creative? If you want to create your very own record-breaking chimera creature, then head to www.guinnessworldrecords.com/2018.

THE CHIMERA!

Here are the record-breaking animals that went into our crazy chimera on pp.28–29. How many were you able to guess?

BODY

Of all the creatures in our mash-up, this is probably the hardest to identify – even when you see the original animal! This fantastic furball is Franchesca, an Angora rabbit from California, USA. Her 36.5-cm-long (1-ft 2.3-in) coat qualifies as the **longest fur on a rabbit**.

HORNS

This breathtaking billy goat is Rasputin from Austria. The gap between the tips of his humongous horns is 135.2 cm (53.2 in) – that's about as wide as the average nine-year-old boy is tall! This makes Rasputin the proud owner of the **largest horn spread on a goat**.

TAIL

When Keon the Irish wolfhound is happy, everyone knows about it because his tail is a force of nature! Measuring 76.8 cm (30.2 in), his wagger is the **longest tail on a dog**. Two-thirds of all the hounds to ever hold this record were the same breed as Keon; the remainder were Great Danes.

EYES

You don't have to look hard to spot this critter's superlative feature... With a body length of up to 16 cm (6.3 in) and 1.6-cm-wide (0.6-in) eyes, the Philippine tarsier has the **largest mammal eyes** in relation to body size. If the tarsier were scaled up to the height of a human, this primate would have eyes the size of grapefruits! You can see more eye-popping animals on pp.36–37.

EARS

Listen up! Harbor the coonhound has the **longest ears on a living dog**. His left and right lugs are 31.1 cm (12.2 in) and 34.3 cm (13.5 in), respectively.

TONGUE

When it comes to tongues, Mochi the St Bernard from South Dakota, USA, has the competition licked. Measured at 18.58 cm (7.3 in) – the same as two-and-a-half Jenga blocks in a row – hers was verified as the **longest tongue on a dog (current)** in 2016.

NOSE

Who *nose* the owner of this humongous hooter? The proboscis monkey has the **longest primate nose**, at roughly the same length as a hot dog! Find out more about this creature on p.34.

ON THE SCENT...

A three-month-old southern tamandua hitches a ride with its mother. Native to South America, these furry, nocturnal creatures are a type of anteater. They spend most of their time foraging in treetops for ants and termites. They have huge tongues – some 40 cm (16 in) in length; that's longer than two hot-dog sausages! Tamanduas may look cute and cuddly, but you don't want to get too close: they emit a strong, musky smell to mark their territory. Hold your nose and turn to pp.48–49 for more stinky specimens!

WILD THINGS

SUPER SNOUTS

The **longest human nose** belongs to Mehmet Özyürek (right) from Turkey, measuring 8.8 cm (3.4 in). But in the battle of the snouts, these creatures blow away all the competition!

①

②

An elephant's trunk contains some 150,000 muscle "fascicles" (bundles of muscle fibre).

③

Be sure to check out the proboscis monkey in our chimera on pp.28–31!

LOL

WHAT DID ONE EYE SAY TO THE OTHER?

BETWEEN YOU AND ME, SOMETHING SMELLS...

① The **longest primate nose** belongs to the proboscis monkey from Borneo. Its appendage can reach 17.5 cm (6.8 in), most commonly in elderly male monkeys. As well as making their honking calls louder, it also turns red to indicate agitation or excitement.

② The world's **largest land mammal** can certainly blow its own trumpet. It boasts the **heaviest nose**, weighing up to 200 kg (440 lb 14 oz). An African elephant's trunk is the **most muscular nose**, too; beyond smelling, it's also used as a tool for eating and lifting objects.

③ Noses don't come much weirder than this... The 22 mini tentacles at the end of the star-nosed mole's snout are packed with nerve endings. This makes it six times more sensitive than a human hand. In fact, it's the **most sensitive animal organ**.

4

All right, who ate baked beans last night?!

7

Whoever smelt it dealt it!

5

FAST FACT

What colour is a polar bear's fur? White is *not* the answer. It's actually transparent. This allows more sunlight to be absorbed by its black skin. Like its sense of smell, this is another adaptation to survive in the frozen Arctic.

6

Elephant seals can hold their breath underwater for two hours!

7

DATA FILE

COMMON NAME:
Southern elephant seal

SCIENTIFIC NAME:
Mirounga leonina

TYPE: Mammal

LOCATION: Argentina, subantarctic islands, Antarctica

LENGTH: 5 m (16 ft 4 in)

④ When you live in the vast, barren wilderness of the Arctic Circle, it pays to be able to pinpoint your next meal from afar. Polar bears can sniff out prey such as seals over 30 km (18 mi) away! Among land mammals, this bear has the **most powerful sense of smell**.

⑤ Weighing 700 g (1 lb 8 oz), the grey-faced sengi from Tanzania is the **largest elephant shrew**. Its long nose isn't the only thing it shares with its namesake. Scientifically speaking, sengis are more closely related to elephants than they are to true shrews!

⑥ This cute bug is an acorn weevil, commonly found living on oak trees. At the end of what looks like its snout – but is actually something called a "rostrum" – is its mouth! It's a feature shared by all weevils, whose 60,000-plus species make up the **largest animal family**.

⑦ The 3,500-kg (7,720-lb) southern elephant seal is not just the **largest pinniped** but also the **largest member of the carnivore family**. When staking a claim to mates or territory, the male inflates its trunk-like proboscis to amplify its roar and scare off rivals.

HERE'S LOOKING AT YOU, KID!

Jeepers, creepers... where'd you get those peepers?! Almost every animal has eyes, but they've evolved in many different ways. As you'll see from these record-breakers, they're as varied and as fascinating as the creatures themselves.

Slit pupils are common to many nocturnal critters, including geckoes, foxes and cats.

This was my shocked face when I found out I was a record-breaker!

FAST FACT

Big eyes are a common trait among deep-sea creatures. The lower layers of the ocean receive very little to no natural light, so supersized eyes help animals to seek out food and companions.

1 "Seed shrimp" – aka Gigantocypris – are small, ball-shaped crustaceans about the same size as a gobstopper. They live in the ocean as deep as 1.3 km (0.8 mi). Their peepers work like mirrors, reflecting the faintest of glimmers to give them the **best night vision** of any animal.

2 The **best *colour* night vision**, on the other hand, belongs to the helmeted gecko from Africa. It's estimated that it can perceive colour 350 times better than humans! It's the first known vertebrate (i.e., creature with a backbone) that can detect colour in the dark.

3 Relative to body size, the aptly named big-eye thresher shark has the **largest eyes for a shark**. Some specimens have eyeballs that span 4% of their body length – up to 16.8 cm (6.6 in) across. In an average-sized man, that would equate to eyes as big as tennis balls!

8 KM

The mantis shrimp is one to look out for in more ways than one... It also packs the **strongest punch** of any animal!

④

⑤

⑥

⑦

DATA FILE

COMMON NAME:
Atlantic giant squid

SCIENTIFIC NAME:
Architeuthis dux

TYPE: Mollusc

LOCATION: Deep oceans

LENGTH: 13 m (42 ft 7 in)

EYE DIAMETER:
Up to 40 cm (15.7 in)

40 CM

④ The peregrine falcon has the **best vision for a bird**, able to spot its dinner from 8 km (5 mi) away! Once in its sights, the victim – usually a bird such as a pigeon – stands little chance. Able to plummet at 300 km/h (186 mph), this ace aviator is also the **fastest bird in a dive**.

⑤ Colour plays a big role in the world of the peacock mantis shrimp – and we're not just talking about its flamboyant shell. With as many as 16 different colour receptors, it boasts the **most sophisticated eyes**. By contrast, humans have just three receptors: red, green and blue.

⑥ The ogre-faced gladiator spider hunts under darkness, so good night vision comes in handy. Like a lot of arachnids, it has eight eyes but only one pair is enlarged. Its two 1.4-mm (0.05-in) eyeballs are the **largest eyes for a spider**. This spider can see better at night than cats and owls.

⑦ Putting all other eyes to shame are the prodigious peepers of the Atlantic giant squid. An eye found in 1878 from one of these elusive deep-sea dwellers was a monstrous 40 cm (15.7 in) across! That's wider than this book when open! It's the **largest eye** of any animal ever recorded.

ANIMAL SUPER POWERS

INTRODUCING... THE ANIMAL INCREDIBLES! WHETHER IT'S SHEER STICKING POWER, MARVELLOUS MIGHT OR SHAPE-SHIFTING GENIUS, THESE WONDER-CREATURES HAVE EVOLVED EXTRAORDINARY ABILITIES TO ENSURE THAT THEY SURVIVE ANOTHER DAY...

SCARAB BEETLE

DUNG BEETLES AND THEIR KIND ARE THE "INCREDIBLE HULKS" OF THE ANIMAL KINGDOM. MEMBERS OF THE SCARAB FAMILY – WHICH ALSO INCLUDES GOLIATH AND RHINOCEROS BEETLES – CAN BEAR AS MUCH AS 850 TIMES THEIR OWN WEIGHT AND PULL AS MUCH AS 1,141 TIMES THEIR OWN WEIGHT! THIS EASILY MAKES THEM THE **STRONGEST INSECTS**.

By burying manure, dung beetles play a vital role in nourishing soil and reducing numbers of flies.

HAIRY FROG

THE **FURRIEST FROG** IS THE MALE HAIRY FROG, WHICH DURING THE MATING SEASON GROWS THICK "HAIR" ON ITS SIDES AND LIMBS. IN REALITY, THESE ARE SKIN FILAMENTS THAT ACT LIKE GILLS IN WATER... THIS SPECIES IS ALSO KNOWN AS THE...

..."WOLVERINE FROG". LIKE THE X-MEN LEGEND (ABOVE), THESE FROGS CAN PRODUCE "CLAWS" FROM UNDER THEIR SKIN. THEY DO THIS BY INTENTIONALLY BREAKING THE BONES IN THEIR TOES!

GECKO

Gecko toes are so sticky because they bond with surfaces at the atomic level.

JUST LIKE SPIDER-MAN, GECKOES CAN CLIMB SMOOTH WALLS AND EVEN SCUTTLE ACROSS CEILINGS. HOWEVER, THEY DON'T NEED ANY WEBBING TO DEFY GRAVITY. THEIR ADHESIVE TOE PADS ARE COVERED IN MILLIONS OF MICROSCOPIC HAIRS THAT CREATE AN ELECTROMAGNETIC ATTRACTION WITH THE SURFACE. IT'S A STICKY BUSINESS!

MIMIC OCTOPUS

THE MIMIC OCTOPUS RIVALS MYSTIQUE (FAR RIGHT) FROM X-MEN FOR ITS SUPERLATIVE SHAPE-SHIFTING ABILITIES. BY CHANGING ITS COLOUR, FORM AND BEHAVIOUR, IT CAN IMPERSONATE AT LEAST 16 DIFFERENT ANIMALS, INCLUDING SEA SNAKES, JELLYFISH AND FLATFISH (ABOVE). NO WONDER IT'S THE **GREATEST OCTOPUS MIMIC!**

ARCHER FISH

HAWKEYE OF THE AVENGERS IS ONE SHARP SHOOTER, BUT SO IS THE APTLY NAMED ARCHER FISH. BY SHAPING ITS MOUTH INTO A NARROW CHANNEL, IT CAN SQUIRT A JET OF WATER TO STRIKE AN UNSUSPECTING INSECT RESTING ABOVE THE WATER. THE **FARTHEST RANGE FOR AN ARCHER FISH** IS 1.5 M (4 FT 11 IN) – MORE THAN SEVEN TIMES ITS OWN BODY LENGTH!

IF YOU'VE GOT IT...

...flaunt it! Brightly coloured creatures are some of the animal world's standout stars. They can use their hues to warn off predators, hide themselves or attract a potential mate.

①

FAST FACT
Evidence from scientific studies suggests that the more eyespots a peacock has in his tail, the more success he will have in finding a female mate (called a peahen).

I wonder if pink's really my colour...

②

③

① A peacock fanning his tail or "train" has to be the best-known example of showing-off in the animal kingdom. The green peacock from south-east Asia is the **largest peafowl species**. Males measure up to 3 m (9 ft 10 in) long – most of which is tail!

② The Australian peacock spider is so-called because of its colourful courtship display. To impress a potential mate, the male waves a patterned, flap-like extension on its abdomen. But if he continues his dance when the female is uninterested, she may attack and even eat him!

③ The pink orchid mantis from Malaysia looks just like – you guessed it – a pink orchid! Its legs mimic the beautiful flower petals, camouflaging it from predators such as birds. They also help to disguise this beautiful bug from its own prey.

QUICK QUIZ

Q. WHAT GIVES FLAMINGOS THEIR PINK COLOUR?

A. A DIET OF SHRIMP

⑤

④

⑥

I told you we were going to clash!

⑦

The brighter the butt, the higher the rank a mandrill has in his troop!

④ As well as being the **largest monkey**, the mandrill is also one of the most colourful mammals. They have blue-and-red faces, and their rumps are red, pink, blue and purple! The hues are more intense in dominant males, and fade if another monkey takes charge of the troop.

⑤ With its eye-popping plumage and curly tail, this Wilson's bird of paradise is dressed to impress. In the gloom of the rainforest floor, the Indonesian native dances and flashes his vibrant feathers at the brown-coloured female, hoping to catch her attention.

⑥ Male and female mandarinfish are as colourful as each other. This Pacific Ocean dweller was named after the vivid robes of a "mandarin", an official in imperial China. It's one of only two vertebrates that produce blue pigment, rather than *appearing* blue by a trick of the light.

⑦ Like some other marine creatures – including the mandarinfish – the sea slug's vivid colouring screams "toxic!". It's a brilliant defence against would-be enemies. Predators would get a very nasty shock if they tried to make a meal of this poisonous mollusc!

TOOL TALES

Humans aren't the only ones that use tools... There are many animals who take advantage of objects from their environment. These smart critters have learned it's not just the early bird that catches the worm, but the bird with the right tool for the job!

CHIMPANZEE

The practice of using a stone as a hammer, as this chimp is doing, dates back at least 4,300 years. It's considered the **earliest tool use by chimpanzees**, since similar "hammers" from the Stone Age were found in the rainforest of the Ivory Coast in Africa. Chimps are also the **first animals to use tools to hunt a land vertebrate**. A group in Senegal, Africa, were seen to dislodge bushbabies from trees with sticks they had sharpened with their teeth. The primates are handy with other props, too, such as using plant stems to scoop water from holes (below).

Chimps can use stone hammers as heavy as 9 kg (19 lb 13 oz).

MUGGER CROCODILE

The **first documented use of tools by reptiles** is a cunning one: in 2007 it was confirmed that mugger crocodiles in India hide themselves in the water with sticks resting on their heads. An unwitting bird comes along to pick up the sticks for its nest and... snap!

NO WAY!

A croc's bite force can rival that of a *T. rex*!

HAWAIIAN CROW

Hawaiian crows are extinct in the wild, but in special breeding facilities they have been observed using sticks to prise bits of food out of holes in logs. They can even re-shape the tool if it's not working!

HYACINTH MACAW

The **longest species of parrot** is the hyacinth macaw, which can grow to 1 m (3 ft 3 in). Native to South America, the colourful bird has a neat way of cracking nuts. It wraps a piece of leaf around the nut to get a better grip, then breaks it open with its strong beak.

Tree frogs have specialized toe pads with great clinging power.

Mothers pass down their tool-using knowledge to their offspring.

ORANG-UTAN

Intelligent orang-utans use plants in lots of inventive ways. Leafy branches serve as umbrellas (above), as well as tools for gathering honey and insects. Some orang-utans wear leaves as gloves to protect them from spiny fruit, or make cushions for sitting in spiky trees.

DUMPY TREE FROG

You would have thought that frogs are quite happy to get wet, wouldn't you? But not this dumpy tree frog. It was snapped in Jakarta, Indonesia, hopping among gerberas (daisies). It climbed a stem to get to the driest part just under the petals and then held the flower over its head until the shower passed.

BEASTS THAT BUILD

Animal architects have developed some ingenious techniques to build their homes. Human engineers can learn a thing or two from these industrious creatures.

POND

LODGE

DAM

FAST FACT

Beavers don't live in dams. Their actual homes are called lodges, which they build in the flooded area, or pond, created by their dams.

GORILLA

Birds aren't the only animals to build nests: a few mammals are also known to make them when they want to catch some "z"s. The **largest nesting mammal** is the gorilla, which can weigh 220 kg (485 lb). Not surprisingly, theirs is also the **largest mammalian nest**, spanning 1.5 m (4 ft 11 in) across the forest floor.

Gorillas don't like to sleep in the same bed twice. They tend to make a fresh one daily.

A beaver's incisor teeth can grow to 25 mm (0.9 in) long!

BEAVER

Beavers gather sticks, stones and mud to build their dams in streams. The resulting ponds serve as defensive moats. The **longest beaver dam** measures some 850 m (2,788 ft), but there are reports of even longer ones!

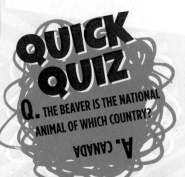

QUICK QUIZ

Q. THE BEAVER IS THE NATIONAL ANIMAL OF WHICH COUNTRY?

A. CANADA

ORANG-UTAN

Although male orang-utans prefer to sleep on the ground like gorillas do (see opposite), the females and their young often create nests in the treetops. Weighing around 37 kg (81 lb), these Indonesian apes are the **largest arboreal (tree-dwelling) mammals**.

TERMITE

The skyscrapers of the animal kingdom are built by some of its smallest members. Incredibly, the visible mounds made by termites are just the tip of the iceberg, serving as chimneys to ventilate nests that extend several metres underground. The **tallest termite mound** – found in the Republic of the Congo – stood 12.8 m (42 ft) above the ground!

BOWERBIRD

While other animal architects build out of necessity, bowerbirds do it for love. The males of this bird family from Australia and New Guinea construct elaborate nests, decorated with colourful objects such as feathers and bottle caps, to try to woo a female.

I wonder if it has a Jacuzzi...

NO WAY!
A termite queen can lay 30,000 eggs per day!

BIG PICTURE

COLOSSAL CHAMELEON

The Parson's chameleon is the world's **largest chameleon**, reaching a length of 68 cm (26.7 in) head to tail – about the same as a domestic cat! It's only found in Madagascar. The African island is home to nearly half of all chameleon species, including the **smallest chameleon** (see opposite). No two Parson's chameleons are exactly alike, with markings and colouration varying across regions. Like all members of this lizard family, it's also able to change colour as a means of communication and temperature control, as well as for camouflage.

FAST FOOD

The early bird may catch the worm, but for chameleons it's the fastest tongue that catches the bug! While this unlucky frog was eyeing up his next meal, a chameleon used his lightning-quick licker to snatch the snack from right in front of him. As well as speed, chameleon tongues have length in their favour; they can reach twice as long as the lizards' bodies!

CHAMELEON

DRAGONFLY

FROG

On average, the *Brookesia micra* is only 16 mm (0.6 in) long from snout to vent, making it the **smallest chameleon**.

100%

16 mm

SMELLY BEASTS

There are some pungent animals out there who literally make a stink to mark territory, defend themselves or even to find a mate! Whatever the reason, you don't want to be caught downwind from these guys...

1

FAST FACT

The hoatzin is the only bird with a digestive system that ferments vegetation as a cow does. It also has a large rubbery callus attached to its breastbone, which acts as a counterweight to stop it falling over when its stomach is too full!

2

3

Wolverines have a strong sense of smell and can detect prey 20 ft (6 m) under the snow!

1 The hoatzin inhabits the Amazon rainforest and is known locally as the "stinky turkey". It is, in fact, the world's **smelliest bird**. Its diet consists mainly of leaves, which are fermented in its large "crop" (a pouch near the throat). That accounts for its manure-like pong!

2 Measuring about 1 m (3 ft 3 in) in length, the wolverine is the **largest weasel**. Like its relatives, this beast sprays a musky scent to mark its territory. If a wolverine fancies saving food for later, it will spray the scraps to put others off. That's one way to make sure nobody steals your lunch!

3 The bombardier beetle is so-named for its impressive defence mechanism. Under threat, the insect spurts a hot, chemical spray from the tip of its abdomen (inset). Containing hydrogen peroxide, the noxious liquid can be fatal to attacking insects.

When I smell this good, how could any lady resist?

4

5

A skunk can fire its foul-smelling spray as far as 10 ft (3 m), so keep your distance!

6

7

They always stop laughing when it's bathtime...

NO WAY!

A hyena's laugh can be heard 8 mi (12.8 km) away!

4 Musk is a smelly substance produced in certain glands by some animals – which is how the musk ox got its name. The males of this Arctic tundra-ranging species emit a powerful odour during the summer mating season to, erm, *attract* females.

5 The striped skunk is the **smelliest mammal**. Startle this creature and it will raise its tail and fire a stinky liquid in your face. The aroma is so potent that it can be detected by humans at an incredibly low dilution – equivalent to one teaspoonful in a swimming pool of water!

6 A type of anteater, the tamandua produces a malodorous musk in its behind. The long-nosed creature marks territory by smearing the pungent stuff on rocks, trees and fallen logs. If attacked, it relies not on its stink but on its sharp claws and powerful forearms.

7 Wanna be in my gang? If you're a spotted hyena, you need the clan scent. Pouches at their rear contain a pongy paste that they rub on to objects and each other to aid communication. The stinky scavengers have powerful digestive systems that can break down almost anything – even bones and hooves!

CAMOUFLAGE

Now you see it, now you don't...
Here are a few amazing animals that perform vanishing acts. The question is: can *you* find them? There's no magic involved – just thousands of years of evolution. They may "disappear" for different reasons and by different means, but they have all learned that camouflage can be the key to survival.

①

You'll have a hoot looking for these feathered friends!

FAST FACT
Most of the animals here use camouflage as a defence, but predators use it too. This can vary from a tiger's stripes to a great white shark's dark back/light belly, which make it harder to see from above or below.

②

Can you guess what this caterpillar is pretending to be?

There's a sting in the tail of the **most venomous fish**...

③

TURN TO PAGE 210 FOR ANSWERS

LOL

WHAT'S BLACK AND WHITE AND RED ALL OVER?

A ZEBRA WITH SUNBURN!

4

This reef-dwelling creature is feeling a little *horse*...

5

This bug *sticks* out more than you might think...

6

You'll want to *leaf* this one alone if you're afraid of big bugs!

7

This mountain inhabitant is the **highest-living predator on land**.

SURFIN' USA

The Surf City Surf Dog competition has been drawing water-loving canines since 2009. Dozens of pooches from as far away as Australia and Brazil gather at Huntington Beach in California, USA, to test their skills against the waves. Here, Tillman the bulldog – who formerly achieved the **fastest 100 m on a skateboard by a dog** – is shown in action at the 2014 event. See who was 2016's top dog and meet more animal surfers on pp.58–59.

ON THE MOVE

BIG PICTURE

SUPER SCOOTER

Norman the Scooter Dog lived up to his name by setting the **fastest 30 m on a scooter by a dog** in 2013. He rolled his way into the record books with a lightning-quick time of 20.77 sec. He rests his front paws on the handlebars and uses one back paw to propel himself forward. Norman, who is owned by Karen Cobb (USA, above), is a Briard – a type of herding dog known for its keen intelligence and memory.

FAST FACT

Norman attended 2016's World Dog Awards along with other famous pooches, including social media stars Doug the Pug and Manny the Frenchie. Norman won the "Top Trick" gong for his cycling skills (see below).

ON YER BIKE!

Norman is no one-trick pooch. As if taming a scooter weren't enough, he also rides a bike. In 2014, he achieved the **fastest 30 m on a bicycle by a dog** – 55.41 sec – in Los Angeles, California, USA (see him in action below). Owner Karen said that Norman nailed how to cycle – with stabilizers – in 10 weeks.

BEASTLY BOARDERS

Animals from all over the globe have taken to skateboards – demonstrating they're as comfortable on four wheels as they are on four paws (or hooves)! Meet the *wheelie* special riders who earned a record or two along the way...

On your marks, get set, *go-at*!

If you ever pass through Fort Myers in Florida, USA, and think you see a goat on a skateboard, don't panic – you're not losing your marbles. The city is home to the Tony Hawk of the goat world: Happie, who rolled 36 m (118 ft) – the **farthest distance skateboarded by a goat**. The Cooke family, who own the Nigerian dwarf cross, think she could have travelled a lot farther, but unfortunately she ran into a parking barrier!

Animals may have been boarding for longer than you think... This ceramic sculpture of a dog riding on a wheeled platform was unearthed in Veracruz, Mexico, and dates to 450–650 CE.

LOL

WHY ARE GOATS SO DIFFICULT TO TALK TO?

BECAUSE THEY'RE ALWAYS BUTTING IN!

Border collie Jumpy is a "stunt dog" with a mind-boggling range of daring skills. As well as backflipping, diving and surfing, he also skateboards. In 2013, he completed the **fastest 100 m on a skateboard by a dog**: 19.65 sec!

Jumping over a bar while riding a skateboard is just *one* of the skills that Didga – short for Didgeridoo – lays claim to. Along with her owner, Robert Dollwet (USA), the multitalented rescue cat holds the record for **most tricks performed by a cat in one minute**: 24. Learn more about this fantastic feline's full repertoire of tricks on pp.112–13.

Jumpy's owner, Omar von Muller, also trained Uggie – the terrier from the movie *The Artist* (2011).

Having already taught mice how to surf (left), animal trainer Shane Willmott from Australia made the leap to skateboarding. He built a mini board and ramp for Harvey (above) and the rad rodent fearlessly rose to the challenge!

Otto the bulldog skilfully glided between 30 pairs of legs on 8 Nov 2015 to achieve the **longest human tunnel skateboarded through by a dog**. On receiving his record, he instantly became a global superstar. He was a contender for "Hot Dog" at 2016's World Dog Awards, but lost out to Dally the Jack Russell, who rides a horse!

Otto rode his skateboard on a downhill path through a park in Lima, Peru.

SURF'S UP!

LOL

WHICH BREED OF DOG MAKES THE BEST SURFER?

THE *BOARD-ER* COLLIE!

These beastly boarders prove that four legs are just as good as two when it comes to surfing. A couple have even carved out records on the crest of a wave!

KELPIE

Say "aloha" to Abbie Girl, the surfing rescue dog from California, USA. Although she lives in the USA, Abbie is an Australian kelpie, which is a type of sheepdog. She pulled off the **longest open-water wave surfed by a dog** – a distance of 107.2 m (351 ft 8 in) – in 2011.

NO WAY!

Kelpies can "surf" on the backs of sheep in a herding trick called "sheep-backing".

LABRADOR

Abbie Girl isn't the only pooch ruling the waves. Labrador Bono, along with his Brazilian owner Ivan Moreira, glided 1.69 km (1.05 mi) up the Mearim River in Arari, Maranhão, Brazil, on 10 Mar 2016. This was the **longest stand-up paddleboard ride on a river bore by a human/dog pair**. River bores are surges of water that can travel inland for miles, allowing surfers to catch a wave far from the beach. They occur during very high tides.

FAST FACT

Bono (right) showed off his skills at the Surf City Surf Dog competition held at Huntington Beach in California, USA, in Sep 2016. He surfed away with first prize, so the judges must have been impressed!

GUINNESS WORLD RECORDS

ALPACA

Domingo Pianezzi from Peru has taught everything from cats to parrots to surf. In 2010, an alpaca called Pisco became his pupil. Pianezzi was inspired to train the Peruvian native after attending an Australian surfing contest, at which he saw riders with koalas and kangaroos.

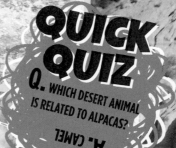

QUICK QUIZ

Q. WHICH DESERT ANIMAL IS RELATED TO ALPACAS?

A. CAMEL

PIG

Pigs may not be able to fly, but nobody said anything about surfing! Hailing from the original home of the surfboard – Hawaii – Kama regularly *hogs* the limelight on trips to the beach with his owner Kai Holt (USA).

You can follow Kama's exploits on YouTube, Facebook and Instagram.

Whatever floats your goat, I guess...

GOAT

"Goat whisperer" Dana McGregor introduced Goatee (far right) to water at an early age. It clearly paid off as she's now an accomplished surfer. Here she is accompanied by one of her "kids", Pismo, who learned the art of catching waves from his mother. The gnarly nanny and her offspring are a common sight on Pismo Beach in California, USA, where Dana runs a surfing school and summer camps for humans, too.

HITCHING A RIDE

Sometimes it's nice to sit back and let someone else take the strain. While at first glance all of these animal hitchhikers look like they're doing just that, the reality can be a little different...

Watch my shell with those talons, I've just had it waxed!

①

②

③

Male rhinoceros beetles use their elaborate horns when battling for a female!

① *Yee-ha*! This Reinwardt's flying frog seems to think it's a cowboy – though there are no reins on the rhinoceros beetle it's riding. Snapped by photographer Hendy Mp in Indonesia, the fearless frog rode the big bug for around five minutes.

② A Galápagos hawk surveys the territory from the vantage point of a giant tortoise's back. Given a chance, this bird of prey would make a meal of a baby tortoise. However, it stands no chance with an adult – the Galápagos giant is the world's **largest species of tortoise**.

③ Three remoras, aka suckerfish, catch a free ride on a green sea turtle in Mexico. A cup-like pad on their heads has powerful suction, enabling them to cling on to larger marine animals. It's great for getting around using the minimum effort.

④ Richard du Toit snapped this impala at a watering hole in Kruger National Park, South Africa. It looks perfectly at ease with seven oxpeckers on its back – and why wouldn't it? The birds rid the antelope of pests, such as ticks, and they get a free lunch!

An oxpecker can eat up to 100 ticks and 12,000 tick larvae per day!

You sit back and relax – I'll take the reins from here, okay?

NO WAY!
Hekan helps to train horses for movies!

In some agricultural parts of India, it's believed that giving frogs a "wedding ceremony" will bring on the rainy season!

(5) Yes, this really is a weasel riding a woodpecker! The extraordinary moment captured by Martin Le-May while walking in a park went viral in 2015. As fun as it looks, there's a darker story playing out here. It's generally thought that the weasel must have attacked the bird just as it was taking off.

(6) Hekan the border collie regularly lends a helping paw at his owners' equestrian centre in Melbourne, Australia. Steve Jefferys and Sandy Langsford are only too glad to let the trusty young sheepdog saddle up and take Kiko the horse for a ride!

(7) You may have heard of a piggyback, but what about a *froggy*back? This lucky mouse got one after it fell into a flooded river in India. Monsoons can make life perilous for land-dwellers, but this amphibious taxi got his passenger home and dry.

BIG PICTURE

GUINNESS WORLD RECORDS

BERTIE

OFFICIALLY AMAZING

FAST-TRACK TORTOISE

Everyone's heard the tale of the tortoise and the hare. It was enough to inspire Bertie to take to the track on 9 Jul 2014. He completed a predetermined course in a time of 19.59 sec at Adventure Valley in Brasside, Durham, UK. This equated to an average speed of 0.28 m/s (0.92 ft/s) – or 1 km/h (0.62 mph) – making Bertie the **fastest tortoise** in the world. This smashed the previous record of 0.45 km/h (0.28 mph), which had stood for nearly 40 years.

FAST FACT

Bertie is a leopard tortoise, a species that grazes on the savannah of southern and eastern Africa. It is one of the planet's biggest tortoises, growing up to 70 cm (27.5 in) long.

NATURE'S SLOW POKES!

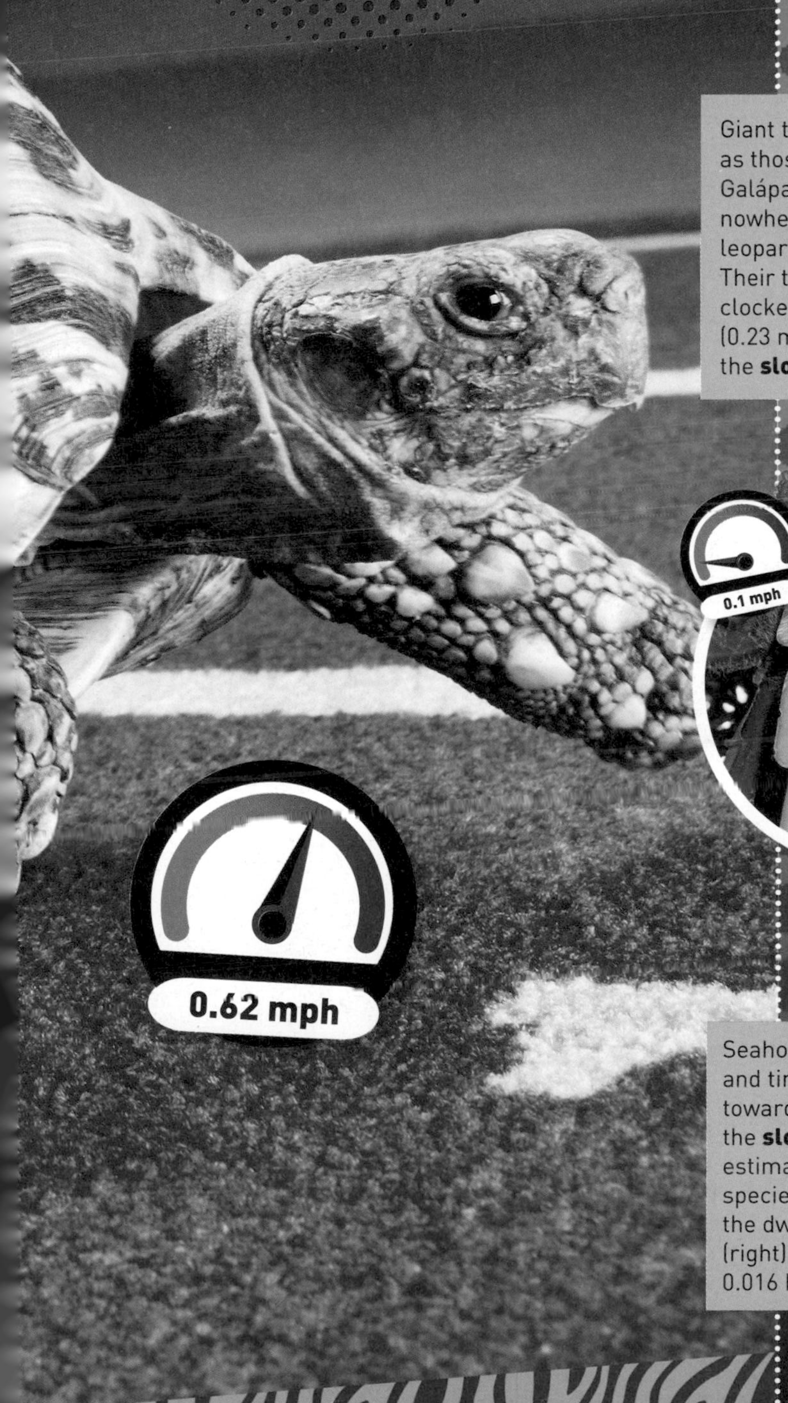

Giant tortoises – such as those from the Galápagos islands – are nowhere near as zippy as leopard tortoise Bertie. Their top speed has been clocked at just 0.37 km/h (0.23 mph), making them the **slowest chelonian**.

0.23 mph

0.1 mph

Notorious for its laid-back lifestyle, the three-toed sloth is regarded as the **slowest mammal**. On the ground, its maximum speed is 0.16 km/h (0.1 mph).

0.62 mph

Seahorses' rigid bodies and tiny fins contribute towards them being the **slowest fish**. It's estimated that smaller species, such as the dwarf seahorse (right), never exceed 0.016 km/h (0.001 mph).

0.001 mph

WHEN DOGS FLY...

Why go walkies in the park when you can glide among the clouds? These parachuting pooches and hang-gliding hounds know that flying isn't just for birds. No wings? No problem – you just need to get your owner on board...

On landing, Arrow springs into action to chase down poachers!

ARROW

A two-and-a-half-year-old German shepherd became the **first skydiving anti-poaching dog** on 17 Sep 2016. Arrow parachuted with his handler, Henry Holsthyzen (left), from a helicopter flying 6,000 ft (1,828 m) above Air Force Base Waterkloof in South Africa. He is the first dog to tandem skydive as part of a pioneering programme to apprehend poachers from the sky.

FAST FACT

Dogs have been helping to fight poaching for decades, on the ground and in the air. But Arrow's leap marks the first time a dog and handler have descended by parachute from such a high altitude.

Land over there – I think I just saw a cat!

SHADOW

Australian shepherd Shadow, kitted out in a specially made harness, is seen hang-gliding with his owner, Dan McManus, outside Salt Lake City in Utah, USA. The pair have been flying together for years. Dan first took his four-legged friend along for a ride because Shadow would get distressed when he was left behind on the ground. The high-flying duo haven't looked back since!

GUINNESS WORLD RECORDS

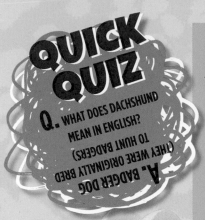

QUICK QUIZ

Q. WHAT DOES DACHSHUND MEAN IN ENGLISH?

A. BADGER DOG (THEY WERE ORIGINALLY BRED TO HUNT BADGERS)

BRUTUS

On 20 May 1997, a daring dachshund made a tandem jump from a plane at 15,000 ft (4,572 m) above sea level – the **highest skydive by a dog**. Brutus, aka the "Skydiving Dog", and his owner, Ron Sirull, flew over the town of Lake Elsinore in California, USA. Ron first decided to take Brutus on his skydives to stop his pet chasing his plane down the runway!

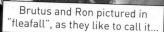

Brutus and Ron pictured in "fleafall", as they like to call it...

TRIXIE

During World War II, thousands of dogs were sent to the front to carry messages and help soldiers locate booby traps. To get behind enemy lines, these heroic hounds sometimes had to make a leap of faith with their human colleagues. One such "paradog" was the US Army's Private Trixie, pictured here with her parachute deployed alongside Sergeant John Patrick. Trixie was the official mascot of the 16th Observation Squadron.

RILEY

Strapped to owner Nathan Batiste with a tailored harness, this daredevil dachshund made his first skydive from 13,000 ft (3,962 m) above California, USA, in 2014. Riley was given his very own "doggles" (bottom right) for the special occasion! After a successful jump, Nathan said: "It was great fun, and the footage of Riley looking around once I'd opened the 'chute is awesome."

NO WAY!

More than 10,000 hounds were trained as part of WWII's "Dogs for Defense" initiative.

Smile for the camera!

Whether accidentally hitching a ride or faithfully following the scent of home, the animals below have all made amazing voyages. But can you untangle their trails to match each wild wanderer with its story?

965,600 KM

The **most well-travelled cat** is Hamlet. In Feb 1984, he escaped from his cage on a flight leaving Toronto, Canada, and became caught behind some plane panelling for more than seven weeks. As a result, the high-flying feline stacked up an estimated 600,000 air miles (965,600 km)!

250 KM

A stray dog in China ran 250 km (155 mi) over the Tian Shan mountains and down to the Gobi Desert along with 101 ultra-marathon competitors in 2016. Gobi – as she came to be called – formed a close bond with one runner in particular, Dion Leonard, who has now given her a home in the UK.

8,046 KM

A Magellanic penguin is thought to swim 5,000 mi (8,046 km) annually to return to the man who saved his life. In 2011, Joao Pereira de Souza found the bird covered in oil on a beach near Rio de Janeiro, Brazil. Ever since, "Dindim" has spent around eight months of each year with Joao, disappearing for the other months, probably to breed farther south.

96 KM

A wild rabbit travelled around 60 mi (96 km) in the UK hidden inside a car bonnet before being discovered. Unable to coax it out, the driver called roadside assistance, who found the runaway under the gearbox! Dubbed "Bugsy", the bunny was released back into the wild.

3,218 KM

The **farthest distance walked home by a dog** was achieved in 1979 by Jimpa, a Labrador-boxer cross. He turned up at his old home in Pimpinio, Victoria, Australia, after walking some 2,000 mi (3,218 km) across the country. His owner had moved with him over a year earlier to Nyabing in Western Australia. That's what you call homesick!

241 KM

It's only right that a guinea pig who hitchhiked 241 km (150 mi) undetected across the UK should be nicknamed "Hitch". Somehow, the rodent got into a bag of hay, which was then put into the back of a car and driven from Kent to Newark. The driver only discovered her after hearing squeaks coming from the sack of hay!

THINKING *INSIDE* THE BOX

Hmm, not quite my size... Maru, who lives in Japan, is famous for trying out bags, boxes and even garbage cans to cosy up in and take a nap. For these and other antics, the beautiful Scottish fold cat is the **most watched cat on YouTube**. Find him and other animal stars from the online world on pp.78–85.

CELEBRITY ANIMALS

MOVIE STARS

Roll out the red carpet for the movie industry's wildest actors! From friendly killer whales to not-so-grizzly bears, these camera-loving critters were happy to take direction. Lights, camera, action!

CRYSTAL

Mischievous monkey Dexter makes life tricky for Larry (played by Ben Stiller, left) in the *Night at the Museum* series. Dexter is actually a capuchin monkey named Crystal, who has appeared in nearly 30 films since her Hollywood career began in 1997. She lives in California, USA, with trainer, Tom Gunderson, and other animal actors.

NIGHT AT THE MUSEUM 2006–14

SALSA & CHIP

After losing his tongue, mute pirate Cotton trains his parrot to speak for him in the first three *Pirates of the Caribbean* films. In reality, the bird was played by *two* blue-and-gold macaws: Salsa and Chip. With treats and clickers, they were taught to act alongside Johnny Depp and others, moving their beaks to simulate talking, and even perching on Cotton's shoulder during sword fights!

PIRATES OF THE CARIBBEAN 2003–07

KEIKO

Since a young age, Keiko the killer whale had only known life in a series of water parks – until he landed the title role in *Free Willy*. He is seen here sharing a joke with his co-star Jason James Richter (Jesse), who befriends him in the story. Willy finds his freedom back in the ocean, and the film inspired a campaign to return Keiko to the wild, too.

FREE WILLY 1993

NO WAY!

Keiko was the first captive orca ever returned to home waters.

FICTIONAL ANIMAL STARS

BART THE BEAR II

Actor Matt Damon may not have thanked trainer Doug Seus for encouraging a grizzly to clamber on to his car (above), but Bart the Bear II was simply doing his job in *We Bought a Zoo*. When not acting in movies, the bear is at home on a Utah ranch with Doug (left) and his wife, Lynne. They adopted the orphaned Alaskan brown bear when he was a cub, along with his sister, Honey Bump. The siblings made their film debuts together in *Dr Dolittle 2* (2001).

WE BOUGHT A ZOO 2011

In 1978, Disney's most iconic star, Mickey Mouse, became the **first fictional character on the Hollywood Walk of Fame** in Los Angeles, California, USA.

MICKEY MOUSE

BLAIR

The **first canine film star** was a collie named Blair. He starred in the 1905 British silent movie *Rescued by Rover*, in which a trusty family dog leads its master to his kidnapped baby. Blair shot to fame after the film's release.

FAST FACT

Blair the collie belonged to *Rescued by Rover*'s producer, Cecil Hepworth, who also played the father in the film. Cecil's wife, Margaret, played the mother and the kidnapped baby was their real daughter.

Woody Woodpecker received his Hollywood star in 1990 – five decades after he was created. The animated bird was based on the acorn and pileated woodpeckers.

WOODY WOODPECKER

RESCUED BY ROVER 1905

Kermit the Frog made it on to the Hollywood Walk of Fame in 2002. The music-making amphibian starred in *The Muppet Show* with fellow well-known characters including Miss Piggy and Gonzo.

Blair and baby Barbara both featured in other films made by Cecil Hepworth.

TOP 10 ANIMAL MOVIES

Some of the all-time greatest blockbuster movies feature big beasts and cute critters. Here, we rank the animal movies that took the biggest bite out of the global box office!

1 JURASSIC WORLD

Dinosaurs may have died out 65 million years ago, but they are still some of the most popular animals in the 21st century. Released in 2015, the fourth instalment in the **highest-grossing dinosaur movie series** came 22 years after the original took the box office by storm (see No.2). The return of the rampaging reptiles attracted total ticket sales of $1,670,328,025 (£1.09 bn) globally. This means that *Jurassic World* is the fifth biggest movie at the cinema of all time.

2 JURASSIC PARK

The original story that laid the scene for *Jurassic World* drew equally big audiences in 1993. Steven Spielberg used a combination of CGI and cutting-edge animatronics to create super-realistic dinos, the likes of which had never been seen. The groundbreaking movie stomped away with $1,038,812,584 (£687.4 m).

3 FINDING DORY

Finding Dory "just kept selling, just kept selling" in 2016, sailing past *Finding Nemo* to become the **highest-grossing underwater movie** of all time. It earned $1,022,617,376 (£809.3 m), making it the second most successful Pixar film to date. At the top spot is 2010's *Toy Story 3*, with takings of $1,069,818,229 (£678.5 m).

4 ZOOTOPIA

One of 2016's biggest animated blockbusters was *Zootopia* (also released under the title *Zootropolis*). The story follows peppy police officer Judy Hopps, who strikes up an unlikely alliance with a fraudster fox to unravel a criminal conspiracy. By the end of its run, the *fur*-nomenal film had grossed $1,019,922,983 (£765.1 m).

5 THE LION KING

This 1994 classic has stood the test of time, even without all the technical wizardry of Disney's more recent offerings (see Nos.3 and 6). The gripping tale of Simba and his fight to rule the African plains earned $987,480,140 (£634.6 m) worldwide. It also inspired one of the most popular stage musicals of all time, which has run on Broadway since 1997 and in London's West End since 1999.

6 THE JUNGLE BOOK

Back in 1967, Disney released a blockbuster animation based on the famous stories by Rudyard Kipling. But its 2016 part-live-action, part-animation version of the wild tale was even more of a roaring success, earning $963,901,123 (£740.8 m). Fans of Mowgli, Baloo and co. will be pleased to hear that another *Jungle Book* movie is in the works – by Warner Bros. – set to hit cinemas in 2018.

7 FINDING NEMO

There was something fishy about this 2003 movie – but it wasn't its box-office performance. The ocean odyssey about an adventure-craving clownfish and his nervy father hauled in a mighty $936,429,370 (£585 m).

8 ICE AGE: CONTINENTAL DRIFT

Like the stars of *Jurassic Park*, none of the beasts in the *Ice Age* series – from mammoths to sabre-toothed cats – are alive today. That hasn't put us off watching them, though. The fourth and most profitable in the series – *Continental Drift* (2012) – took $879,765,137 (£561.8 m).

9 THE SECRET LIFE OF PETS

Ever wondered what the animals in your life get up to when left to their own devices? If this *pet*-acular movie is anything to go by, the answer seems to be: get into lots of mischief! Developed by the makers of *Despicable Me*, the animation was one of 2016's runaway successes. It Max-ed out at $875,958,308 (£714.8 m).

10 ICE AGE: DAWN OF THE DINOSAURS

Just behind *Continental Drift* is the third instalment in the *Ice Age* saga, which earned $859,701,857 (£515.4 m) in 2009. This story kicks off with Manny finding three eggs that hatch into baby *T-rexes*. When the dinos' mother attacks, the gang finds itself trapped in a prehistoric jungle under the ice.

Source: The-Numbers.com; correct as of 20 Jan 2017

DOGS on TV

Whether man's best friend or a mischievous mutt, dogs on television make for heart-warming viewing. From old classics to new hits, here's our round-up of the most iconic small-screen canine stars!

1

Lassie's companion Timmy Martin was played by child actor Jon Provost from 1957 to 1964.

2

Homer and I could do *Dancing with the Stars...*

3

LOL

WHICH IS LASSIE'S FAVOURITE VEGETABLE?

*COLLIE*FLOWER!

1 The much-loved canine character Lassie was the star of a long-running TV series of the same name from 1954 to 1973. Each new Lassie was played by descendants of the first actor – a collie called Pal from the original movie *Lassie Come Home* (1943).

2 In *The Simpsons* – the **longest-running animated sitcom** (it started in 1989) – the family's adopted greyhound doesn't usually live up to his name... Santa's Little Helper is often caught digging holes in the yard or destroying the furniture!

3 "Whenever you're in trouble, just yelp for help!" That's the catchphrase of *PAW Patrol*, a series that follows a pack of rescue dogs led by 10-year-old boy Ryder. With the help of gadgets aplenty, they keep the community of Adventure Bay safe.

④ Stan the dog has a secret: he can talk. And he writes a blog, of course – all about living with two families brought together by a new marriage. Disney's *Dog with a Blog* sees the cheeky collie bring the siblings closer as they work together to conceal his ability.

⑤ If you live in the post-apocalyptic Land of Ooo, as *Adventure Time*'s Finn does, you need a best friend like Jake. A dog with magical powers, Jake can change shape and size at will. Abilities like that come in handy when rescuing the likes of Princess Bubblegum!

What?! What have I done now?

"Scaredy-dog" Scooby-Doo solves mysteries with his owner and best friend, Norville "Shaggy" Rogers.

⑥ Scooby-Doo has been entertaining us since 1969. Always hungry and often terrified, the goofy Great Dane summons courage when his human pals Fred, Velma, Daphne and Shaggy are in danger. With so many mysteries solved and villains caught, he's definitely earned a few "Scooby snacks"!

⑦ Family life can be tough, as Stella from *Modern Family* knows all too well! The French bulldog just can't seem to stay out of trouble... Still, it must be quite an honour to work with Sofía Vergara, who plays her owner, Gloria (inset above). Vergara is currently the **highest-earning TV actress**.

VIDEOGAME STARS

Some of the most famous characters from the world of videogames were inspired by real-life creatures. Find out more about the amazing arcade animals who have been keeping us entertained for years.

Both Donkey Kong and Fox McCloud were created by Japanese game designer Shigeru Miyamoto.

DONKEY KONG

The barrel-throwing gorilla was the baddie in the **first platform videogame**, *Donkey Kong* (1981). He kidnaps the girlfriend of "Jumpman", who we now know as Mario. Real-life male gorillas (example inset below) are the **largest primates** and possess great strength, but only use violence as a last resort.

KNUCKLES

Sadly, there aren't any blue hedgehogs like Sonic... but his pal Knuckles *is* based on the bizarre-looking echidna. Although sometimes called spiny anteaters, this is not biologically accurate. Along with the duck-billed platypus, echidnas are "monotremes" – a primitive group of mammals that lay eggs rather than giving birth to live young.

MADE-UP ANIMALS IN GAMES

CRASH

At first glance, Crash looks a bit like a fox, but he is, in fact, a bandicoot (above). Similarly, bandicoots look like rodents, but are, in fact, marsupials – relatives of kangaroos – from Australasia. When Crash was first being developed, he was based on another marsupial and was known as "Willie the Wombat".

Pokémon takes elements from lots of real animals to create brand-new ones. Sparky star Pikachu looks a little bit like a pika – a cute mountain-dwelling critter related to rabbits.

Trico is one of the largest creatures to appear in a videogame. The griffin-like beast from *The Last Guardian* (2016) is a jumble of a dog, cat and eagle. He's both a loyal pet and a handy way of getting around!

FOX McCLOUD

We first met Fox McCloud in 1993, with the release of the original *Star Fox* game. The ace aviator leads a team of animal pilots, including Peppy Hare and Slippy Toad. The closest thing to McCloud in the real world is not actually a fox but a bat. With a wing-span of 1.7 m (5 ft 7 in), the "flying fox" (above) is, in fact, the world's **largest bat**.

The new-look Fox McCloud appears in *Star Fox Zero* (2016).

While dinosaurs were real animals, Yoshi's species is fictional. His full name is T Yoshisaur Munchakoopas. We definitely don't recall seeing any dinos in boots in *Jurassic World* (2015)!

GUINNESS WORLD RECORDS

Intro by DanTDM

GAMER'S EDITION
THE ULTIMATE GUIDE TO GAMING RECORDS

You can find hundreds more gaming stars and records in *GWR: Gamer's Edition*. This year's book includes a superhero feature chapter, an exclusive Donkey Kong photoshoot and a special feature on Pokémon.

MOST LIKED...

Some of the biggest social-*pet*working stars are cute, comic or uncommonly curious creatures. Here's a handful of the most popular beasts on Facebook as of 3 May 2017...

Go ahead, make my day...

CAT

Tardar Sauce, better known as "Grumpy Cat", is the **most liked cat on Facebook**, with 8,759,819 fans. Since the hilariously moody moggy became an internet hit in 2012, she has made multiple TV and film appearances. She even has her own replica at Madame Tussauds and an app called *Grumpy Cat's Worst Game Ever* (left).

GRUMPY CAT'S WORST GAME EVER

Grumpy Cat has teamed up with Garfield for a comic-book series featuring the grouchy pair.

Rescue cat Lil Bub was born with various medical issues, including dwarfism and her signature protruding tongue. With nearly 3 million Facebook likes, the popular puss raises money for homeless animals worldwide.

Struggling London busker James Bowen and a stray cat met in 2007 and turned each other's lives around. The ginger star has over half a million Facebook likes, and played himself in 2016 movie *A Street Cat Named Bob*.

No explanation required for why Venus the cat has over 1.3 million Facebook likes... The amazing "two-faced" feline was found as a stray in North Carolina, USA. How she came to look this way is still debated by scientists!

GUINNESS WORLD RECORDS

FAST FACT

San Diego Zoo has had some notable escapees over the years. The best known is Ken Allen, a Bornean orang-utan who gained the nickname "Hairy Houdini" for his skill as an escape artist!

ZOO

San Diego Zoo in California, USA, is the **most liked zoo**, with 705,698 thumbs-up on Facebook. Founded in 1916, the wildlife wonderland is home to more than 3,700 rare and endangered animals, including polar bears (right), western lowland gorillas and three giant pandas (on loan from China).

Three bears – Kalluk, Chinook and Tatqiq – inhabit San Diego Zoo's Polar Bear Plunge.

Hairy hound Beast feels right at home on social media. Well, his owners *are* Priscilla Chan and Mark Zuckerberg – co-founder of Facebook, the **largest online social network**. The Puli, aka Hungarian sheepdog, has over 2.6 million likes, and his interests are listed as "cuddling and herding". The breed is famous for its long, corded coat (see far left)!

ANIMATED ANIMAL

The **most likes for an animated animal on Facebook** is shared by legendary rivals Tom and Jerry, who have stacked up 42,788,398 likes between them. The terrible twosome have been playing their classic cat-and-mouse act since 1940, when they were created for MGM.

DOG

Ever-popular pooch Boo is the **most liked dog on Facebook**, with 17,257,906 fans. The 11-year-old Teddy Bear Pomeranian, who has "written" several books about his life, delights fans with adorable photos of himself in assorted T-shirts, or hanging out with his puppy pals. One of these is fellow record-breaking Pom Jiffpom – you can learn all about him over on pp.84–85!

Boo helped sell ice-cream to raise money for an animal shelter in San Francisco, California, USA.

MOST VIEWED...

Feline frolics or canine comedy? Whatever your entertainment of choice, YouTube has some caught-on-camera classics. When logged on 3 May 2017, these were some of the most watched animals from around the globe.

This talented hound even recorded her own song: "Mishka's Ballad".

Let's go right now, cmon let's go

ANIMAL

Mishka the "talking dog" delighted millions of YouTube viewers with her ability to howl phrases such as "I love you" and "I'm hungry". The Siberian husky, who died aged 14 in Apr 2017, is the **most viewed animal**, with her videos racking up 508,474,297 plays. She also has the **most subscribers for an animal**: 860,540. Mishka, which means "teddy bear" in Russian, lived in New Jersey, USA, with her owner, Matt Gardea.

Meet Denver from Maryland, USA. This is his famous guilty face... Videos of the hangdog Lab retriever being confronted about stolen cat food or wrecked Christmas decorations have attracted more than 65 million views.

Mishka would have approved of this YouTube channel... Gone to the Snow Dogs follows the everyday lives of a family of huskies from Michigan, USA. Nearly 88 million people have watched their antics to date.

Viewers can't get enough of Maymo and his adventures. Videos of the beagle "fighting" vegetables while dressed as a carrot (above), for example, or taking shopping trips with his sister Penny, have been seen some 186 million times.

Coyote gets slimed by a California black sea hare, the **largest sea slug**!

ANIMAL CHANNEL

Adventurer Coyote Peterson (left) puts the "brave" into Brave Wilderness. His wild antics appear on YouTube's **most watched** and **most subscribed animal channel**, with 859,464,329 views and 6,050,821 subscribers, respectively. Typical videos include Coyote allowing himself to be stung by the **largest wasp** (the tarantula hawk wasp, above right), or taking on an apple-eating contest with the famously aggressive cassowary (left), widely considered the world's **most dangerous bird**.

ANIMATED ANIMAL

The **most viewed animated animal on YouTube** is Simon's Cat, star of a series of short films of that name created by British artist Simon Tofield. With 871,420,371 views, the moggy made his first appearance in a video entitled *Cat Man Do*, in which the ever-hungry feline goes to extreme lengths to get Simon out of bed!

Adjudicator Kaoru Ishikawa presents box-happy Maru with his GWR certificate at his home in Japan

CAT

Full of character and sublimely lazy, Maru is the **most viewed cat on YouTube**. His name means "round" in Japanese, and it's partly his tubbiness that has won the Scottish fold cat so many fans. Videos of Maru getting stuck in various places and containers, or just taking life easy, have been watched 340,280,203 times.

MOST FOLLOWED...

With picture-*purr*fect posts, building a fanbase must have been a walk in the park for these photogenic pets. Check out the most popular "Instagr-animals" as of 3 May 2017...

CAT

Blue-eyed Nala is the **most followed cat on Instagram**, with 3.4 million followers. The six-year-old Siamese-tabby mix from California, USA, has a page of her website dedicated to portraits made by adoring fans (example below).

Nala was adopted from an animal shelter at six months old.

Hamilton the Hipster Cat from California, USA, was adopted as a feral kitten. His owner's snaps of the furry feline (and his magnificent "moustache") were an instant Instagram hit, and he has some 725,000 followers.

Smoothie, a British longhair cat living in the Netherlands, became Insta-famous for her stunning looks. With her jewel-like green eyes, she's considered the world's most photogenic cat by her 976,000 followers.

Snoopybabe, an American shorthair-Persian cross, boasts a loveable "pie face". He often poses in his latest outfit for fans, who number more than 362,000. He has a big following on social media in China, where he lives.

DOG
JIFFPOM

NO WAY!
Jiffpom has met Calvin Harris, Katy Perry, Kevin Hart and Sia!

Jiffpom whizzes around on his own specially made skateboard.

4,800,000 FOLLOWERS

Jiffpom from California, USA, is Instagram's **most followed dog**. The teddy lookalike has appeared in films and on TV, and has many celeb pals. Turn the page for a full profile.

HEDGEHOG
BIDDYTHEHEDGEHOG

523,000 FOLLOWERS

Although he passed away in 2015, Biddy is still the **most followed hedgehog**. The cute African pygmy regularly joined his owners on spectacular hiking trips around Oregon, USA.

PIG
PRISSY_PIG

We really like to ham it up on Instagram!

670,000 FOLLOWERS

Miniature pig Priscilla (left) has the **most followers for a pig**. The Florida-based hog shares her profile with Poppleton (right), two other piggies and even the occasional pug!

FOX
JUNIPERFOXX

1,400,000 FOLLOWERS

Juniper has the **most followers for a fox**. The happy, sock-eating animal lives with her adoptive mother, Jessika, and her canine friend, Moose (see p.179).

RACCOON
PUMPKINTHERACCOON

1,100,000 FOLLOWERS

Pumpkin thinks she's a dog. Instagram's **most followed raccoon** lives in The Bahamas with two *real* dogs – Oreo and Toffee – and their owners Laura and William Young.

FAST FACT
The dark fur around a raccoon's eyes resembles a bandit's mask. This, in addition to their high intelligence and natural curiosity, has given the animals a reputation for mischief!

GETTING TO KNOW...
JIFFPOM

Pawple

AT HOME WITH **JIFFPOM**

Jiffpom takes the weight off his paws and reveals what it's like to be the planet's most popular Pomeranian

"Hi, everyone! It's Jiffpom. People are always *hounding* me on social media to find out what it's like to be one of the world's most famous dogs, so I thought: why not give the readers of *Pawple* a snapshot of my life?

"I'd like to start by saying, I love my job!

I get to appear on primetime TV, hang out with celebrities and share my favourite snaps with fans online. By the way, it was a great honour to be voted social media's Best Animal at the 2016 Shorty Awards. I was sure Doug the Pug would get it!

"But, you know, my life isn't all galas and taking selfies with the stars. I spend a lot of time backstage – and some places don't even provide

Above: Jiffpom demonstrates his fancy footwork as well as a keen eye for fashion

TELEVISION

Hanging out with the presenters on *Good Morning America* in 2014

Pawple

MUSIC VIDEOS

I had to act like I was scared of her, but Katy Perry was lovely to work with on "Dark Horse"

FILM PREMIERES

Getting my vampire on at the opening night of *Hotel Transylvania 2* with Alli Simpson in 2015

on the Kaarster See lake in Kaarst, Germany.

BOOKS

SEE IT 3D WITH THE FREE APP

FACT
Jiff appeared in a Katy Perry video ("Dark Horse", 2013) and in the film *Adventures of Bailey: A Night in Cowtown* (USA, 2013).

3D ON THIS PAGE
Augmented Reality alert!

Fastest 10 m on hind legs by a dog
Jiff the Pomeranian covered 10 m (32 ft) in 6.56 sec at TOPS... in Grayslake, ... The plucky ...icks, can also ...), covering 5 m ...ing, in a record 7.76 sec – the **fastest 5 m on front legs by a dog**.

I first appeared in the 2015 edition of *Guinness World Records*

dog treats! Finding the right outfit in my size can be a nightmare. Plus, you won't believe the number of takes we do sometimes in rehearsal before the director is happy. Still, if I'm honest, I wouldn't change any of it.

"One of my proudest moments, though, has to be setting my first two Guinness World Records titles. It all came about when I discovered I had a hidden talent: walking on two paws!

"Before I knew it, I was the holder of two brand-new records: **fastest 10 m on hind legs by a dog** and **fastest 5 m on front legs by a dog**.

"Talking about making a move, I must dash. I've got to get ready for a movie premiere. I hope my pal Boo is going to be there. Two Poms are always better than one."

AWARDS

As the **most followed dog on Instagram**, it was an honour to accept my 2016 Shorty Award with PrankvsPrank's Jeana Smith and Jesse Wellens

Getting the VIP (very important *paw*-son) treatment at 2015's NYX FACE Awards

Rocking a bow-tie with Griffin Gluck at the 2016 Kids' Choice Awards

GUESS MY PET!

Can you identify which animals belong to these famous faces? Watch out though, as one of these is a trick question! Find the answers on pp.210–11.

CARA DELEVINGNE

2

A **RABBIT**   B **FROG**   C **LIZARD**

WILLIAM & KATE

1

A **HORSE**   B **HAMSTER**   C **MOUSE**

ED SHEERAN

3

A **BEAR**   B **SNAKE**   C **CAT**

MILEY CYRUS

④

| A | DOG | B | PIG | C | CAT |

DanTDM

⑤

| A | BEAGLE | B | PUG | C | POODLE |

QUICK QUIZ

Q. WHICH UNUSUAL PET WAS THE ARTIST SALVADOR DALÍ FAMED FOR KEEPING?

A. AN ANTEATER

REESE WITHERSPOON

⑥

| A | FOX | B | GERBIL | C | DONKEY |

LOL

WHAT DO YOU CALL A CELEBRITY RODENT?

FAMOUSE

BATTY ABOUT BATS

At the Tolga Bat Hospital in Australia, tiny orphaned fruit bats are cared for before being released back into the wild (see pp.96–97). Every afternoon, the baby bats descend from their 6-m-high (20-ft) roosts to be gently wrapped up and bottle-fed. Rescue director Jennefer Maclean and her team also aim to dispel bat myths and show that these intelligent, curious creatures shouldn't be feared but respected.

ANIMAL RESCUES

SUPER-ANIMALS

FORGET SUPERMAN AND WONDER WOMAN – IT'S TIME TO CELEBRATE THE UNSUNG SUPER-CREATURES THAT SAVED THE DAY! FOR SOME, RESCUING HUMANS IS JUST ANOTHER DAY AT THE OFFICE... BUT FOR OTHERS, THEY'RE ORDINARY ANIMALS THAT STEPPED UP TO DO EXTRAORDINARY THINGS FOR PEOPLE IN NEED!

JACK THE BLACK

SAVING LIVES IS PART OF THE DAY JOB FOR NEWFOUNDLAND JACK THE BLACK VOM MUEHLRAD. HE AND HIS HANDLER HANS-JOACHIM BRUECKMANN BOTH WORK FOR A GERMAN SEARCH-AND-RESCUE ORGANIZATION. JACK ACHIEVED THE **FASTEST TIME FOR A DOG TO RETRIEVE A PERSON FROM WATER** IN 2013 (BELOW) – PADDLING 25 M (82 FT) WITH SOMEONE IN TOW IN A SPEEDY 1 MIN 36 SEC!

ORION

ON 15-16 DEC 1999, TERRIBLE STORMS LED TO WIDESPREAD FLOODING AND LANDSLIDES IN THE REGION OF VARGAS IN VENEZUELA. FEARLESS ROTTWEILER ORION AND OWNER MAURICIO PÉREZ MERCADO PLUNGED INTO THE MAYHEM TO HELP LOCALS STRANDED IN THE FLOODWATERS. THEY FERRIED AT LEAST 37 PEOPLE TO SAFETY THROUGH THE NIGHT – THAT'S THE **MOST HUMANS RESCUED BY A DOG IN 24 HOURS.**

BINTI JUA

IN 1996, A THREE-YEAR-OLD BOY FELL INTO THE GORILLA ENCLOSURE AT CHICAGO'S BROOKFIELD ZOO IN ILLINOIS, USA. IT COULD HAVE SPELLED DISASTER – BUT BINTI JUA JUMPED INTO ACTION! CARRYING HER OWN BABY ON HER BACK, THE AMAZING APE KEPT THE OTHER GORILLAS AT BAY. SHE THEN GENTLY PICKED UP THE CHILD (SEE INSET RIGHT) AND CARRIED HIM TO A DOOR, WHERE ZOO STAFF WERE ABLE TO RETRIEVE HIM.

?????

SOMETIMES SUPERHEROES PREFER TO KEEP THEIR IDENTITY A SECRET – LIKE THIS ANONYMOUS MOGGY FROM THE SWISS ALPS... A HUNGARIAN HIKER HAD SPRAINED HIS ANKLE AND BECOME LOST WHILE WALKING IN THE MOUNTAINS. LUCKY FOR HIM, THIS FEARLESS FELINE SHOWED UP AND LED HIM BACK TO CIVILIZATION...

LUDWIG

BURGLARS BREAKING INTO THE HOME OF MIKE MAUGHAN AND LIANE SCHOLZ IN DERBY, UK, CLEARLY WEREN'T BANKING ON RUNNING INTO LUDWIG! HIS OWNERS – WHO HAD BROUGHT THE UNUSUAL PET WITH THEM FROM CANADA – BELIEVE THAT THE GRUNTING OF THEIR POT-BELLIED PIG MUST HAVE SCARED THE INTRUDERS AWAY. THIS SUPER SECURITY SWINE MAY WELL HAVE SAVED THEIR BACON!

WILLIE

WHEN THIS PLUCKY PARROT FROM DENVER, COLORADO, USA, NOTICED THAT A TODDLER WAS CHOKING ON HER BREAKFAST, HE FLAPPED HIS WINGS AND CRIED OUT "MAMA, BABY!" AS A RESULT, WILLIE'S OWNER – WHO WAS BABYSITTING AT THE TIME – CAME RUNNING FROM THE NEXT ROOM AND CLEARED THE CHILD'S AIRWAY. BRAVO, WILLIE, FOR RAISING THE ALARM!

Willie received an Animal Lifesaver Award from the Red Cross for his heroic actions!

SUPER-HUMANS

HOT ON THE HOOVES OF OUR SUPER-ANIMALS (SEE PP.90-91), NOW MEET THE SUPER-HUMANS WHO HAVE RETURNED THE FAVOUR! WHETHER THEY HAVE OPENED THEIR HOMES TO ORPHANS OR FREED CRITTERS STUCK IN WEIRD PLACES, THESE SELFLESS HEROES PROVE THE EPIC LENGTHS THEY'LL GO TO FOR ANIMALS IN NEED.

IN 2006, THE THEN **TALLEST MAN** CAME TO THE AID OF TWO DOLPHINS IN DISTRESS. BAO XISHUN FROM MONGOLIA WAS CALLED IN BY AN AQUARIUM WHEN THE DOLPHINS ATE SOME PLASTIC. HIS LONG ARMS WERE ABLE TO REACH ALL THE WAY INTO THEIR STOMACHS TO RETRIEVE THE PLASTIC AND SAVE THEIR LIVES!

BAO XISHUN

Former **tallest man** Bao Xishun stands an incredible 2.36 m (7 ft 8.9 in) from head to toe!

VIKKIE

I just can't figure out where Fagin's got to...

VIKKIE KENWARD FROM WEST SUSSEX, UK, FOUND FAGIN AS A FLEDGLING IN 2016. THE BABY CROW HAD FALLEN OUT OF A TREE AND HAD BEEN ABANDONED BY HIS MOTHER, SO VIKKIE ADOPTED HIM. EVEN NOW HE IS GROWN UP AND FREE TO LEAVE THROUGH AN OPEN WINDOW, FAGIN IS YET TO FLY THE NEST. HE LIKES TO HANG OUT WITH HIS NEW MUM WHILE SHE WATCHES TV OR DOES THE HOUSEHOLD CHORES, PERCHED ON HER SHOULDER OR HEAD. HE'S EVEN FORMED AN UNLIKELY FRIENDSHIP WITH VIKKIE'S PET DOG, INCA (INSET)!

RSPCA

THE UK'S ROYAL SOCIETY FOR THE PREVENTION OF CRUELTY TO ANIMALS (RSPCA) HAS BEEN HELPING CREATURES IN NEED SINCE 1824. SOME OF THE MOST BIZARRE RESCUES IN 2016 WERE A SEAGULL THAT FELL INTO A POT OF COLD CURRY (ABOVE) AND GOLDFISH FOUND IN A DRAIN (RIGHT)!

SCOTT

AUSTRALIAN POLICE OFFICER SCOTT MASON RESCUED CUEJO NOT ONCE, BUT TWICE! HE RAISED THE ORPHAN AFTER THE JOEY'S MOTHER DIED IN A TRAFFIC ACCIDENT. A FEW WEEKS LATER, AN EAGLE TRIED TO FLY AWAY WITH THE YOUNG KANGAROO WHILE HE WAS PLAYING OUTSIDE THE POLICE STATION. SCOTT CHASED DOWN THE BIRD AND MANAGED TO SAVE CUEJO AGAIN! THE UNLUCKY ROO WAS HURT BUT THANKFULLY ALIVE.

MIKE

WHEN A GOSLING WAS IN DANGER OF BEING RUN OVER BY BOATS ON LAKE OSWEGO IN OREGON, USA, MIKE JIVANJEE LEAPT TO ACTION. HE TOOK THE CANADIAN GOOSE – WHOM HE NAMED KYLE – UNDER HIS WING AND RAISED HER UNTIL SHE COULD FEND FOR HERSELF. THE PAIR NOW SHARE A CLOSE BOND, OFTEN TAKING BOAT TRIPS TOGETHER ON THE LAKE WHERE THEY MET.

TADEUSZ

WHILE WALKING HIS DOG IN POLAND, TADEUSZ ŁUBIARZ DISCOVERED A TINY RED SQUIRREL CLOSE TO DEATH ON THE GROUND. TAKING THE ORPHAN HOME, TADEUSZ FED THE SQUIRREL GOAT'S MILK UNTIL HE'D MADE A FULL RECOVERY. HE NAMED THE WOODLAND CRITTER "PITEK" AFTER THE PIPETTE USED TO FEED HIM.

Now inseparable, Pitek and Tadeusz often walk in the local park together.

ROAR-SOME Rescues

THE WILD ANIMAL SANCTUARY

Set up in 1980, the Wild Animal Sanctuary in Colorado, USA, is a haven for formerly captive creatures from all over North and South America. Its 720 acres (291 ha) are roamed by more than 450 large carnivores and exotic animals. Find out more online at www.wildanimalsanctuary.org.

They bend over backwards to help animals here!

The Wild Animal Sanctuary is home to 183 bears, including brown bears such as Gaika and Nadia (left). Nadia was born on the site, but Gaika lived in a truck for 17 years as part of a Russian circus. He was brought to the sanctuary when the circus closed. Each animal type is allocated a particular habitat across the reserve. Many, like the bears, have seasonal pools and waterfalls for swimming, as well as heated underground dens. Luxury!

As well as grizzlies like these, the sanctuary is also home to Syrian, Asiatic, Kodiak and black bears.

Big cats often have to be saved from private "pet" owners. Lioness Lacie (left, with Arthur) was kept locked up in a horse trailer in Ohio, USA, with her mate and four cubs. The park has welcomed many wild cats over the years, such as tigers (right), leopards, pumas, bobcats, lynx and African servals.

There are currently 55 rescued tigers at the sanctuary.

Large animals often become stressed by the presence of humans. Sanctuary director Pat Craig discovered that if people are on raised platforms, they are not seen by the animals as a threat. Now, visitors can watch the free-roaming wildlife from a 2.34-km footbridge (1.45-mi); it's the **longest elevated walkway in an animal sanctuary**.

The sanctuary welcomes some 200,000 visitors each year, including school children and wildlife photographers.

Kaitlyn the coati is one of two of these raccoon-like omnivores in residence. Their long snouts and tree-climbing abilities help them to hunt lizards, birds and fruit in the wild. Native to the Americas, coatis are sometimes domesticated, however these highly active creatures don't make ideal pets.

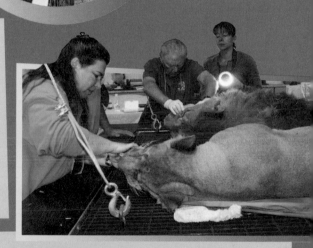

Vets examine newly rescued lions, who will be vaccinated if necessary. The sanctuary includes a rehabilitation centre, where recent arrivals can be acclimatized to their new surroundings and other animals before being released to roam more freely.

NO WAY!

The big cats and wolves eat about 25,000 lb (11,340 kg) of meat every week!

The park counts 17 wolves among its inhabitants. That number includes an unexpected litter of cubs, born shortly after a group of wolves was rescued from a closing zoo. Once adopted by the sanctuary, even a lone wolf has a good chance of running with the pack!

Timber or grey wolves such as these are native to remote areas of Eurasia and North America.

BAT SANCTUARY

The pups are swaddled in blankets to keep them calm and still during feeds. Being placental mammals, they drink milk as babies. They're bottle-fed cow's milk or formula, while fruit is gradually introduced as they mature. It's because of their fruit-based diet that flying foxes are also known as fruit bats.

Adult flying foxes groom themselves frequently with their claws and tongue. Normally, bat mothers would lick their young to keep them clean. Volunteers at the hospital wash and groom the orphans daily, with water, baby wipes and a comb.

Bats are very clean animals that groom themselves as much as cats!

Ever thought a bat could look as cute as this? These spectacled flying foxes are orphans at the Tolga Bat Hospital in Queensland, Australia. At this special sanctuary, the young bats get all the love and attention they need while growing up, before being reintroduced to the wild.

Hey, can I get a refill over here, please?

Bats are social creatures that like to huddle close together in colonies.

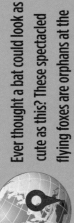

These baby bats (aka pups) are around four weeks old. At this age in the wild, a pup would be carried on its mother's belly, where it can drink her milk. The orphans are given pacifiers as a comforting alternative.

FAST FACT

At night, spectacled flying foxes in the wild "park" their young in nursery trees while they go out searching for food. The baby bats are then picked up in the morning!

Spectacled flying foxes get their name from the light-coloured fur around their eyes.

QUICK QUIZ

Q. WHAT SPEED CAN A FLYING FOX REACH IN FLIGHT?

A. 50 KM/H (31 MPH)

The Tolga Bat Hospital houses anything from 100 to 800 orphans at a time. At around four months old, if fit enough, the bats are released back into the wild. Hospital staff continue to feed them in the forest for another three months, until they can survive on their own.

Flying foxes are the world's **largest bats**, with wing-spans up to 1.7 m (5 ft 7 in). The spectacled species is currently in danger of extinction, owing to habitat loss and disease. Active since 1990, the hospital also treats adult bats affected by tick paralysis. Some orphans are reunited with their mothers, if the parent has recovered well enough to produce milk again and feed its young.

MEDICAL MARVELS

Animal patients benefit as much as anyone from advances in 3D printing and other technologies. New limbs can be conjured from computers, and bionic beasts given back their bounce. Here are some of the veterinary world's superlative success stories...

I've rediscovered my porpoise in life!

WINTER

At just two months old, Winter the bottlenose dolphin lost her tail after becoming entangled in a crab trap. Luckily, she was found and taken to the Clearwater Marine Aquarium in Florida, USA. But without her "flukes", she was unable to swim properly. Over a year and a half, experts designed and tested a brand-new tail, made out of silicone and plastic. Winter's story has inspired books, films and even a videogame. Lessons learned from the making of her prosthetic tail have also been applied to human amputees.

Winter played herself in the 2011 film *Dolphin Tale*, based on her story.

NAKI'O

You can see where Naki'o – which means "puddle" in Hawaiian – got his name. Abandoned as a puppy in a cold basement, he was found with his paws encased in frozen pools of water. Badly frostbitten, they had to be amputated. His adoptive owner, Christie Pace, turned to bionic specialists OrthoPets to design him four prosthetic paws – giving him a real spring in his step!

FAST FACT

The tail flukes, which Winter lost, are a dolphin's powerhouse. They are attached to the "peduncle", the muscular part of the mammal's body. To swim naturally, dolphins move the peduncle up and down, and the flukes then propel them forward.

BUTTERCUP

In Tennessee, USA, Buttercup the duck was born with his left foot turned backwards, leaving him unable to walk – or waddle – properly. Step in 3D-printing company NovaCopy. They scanned the foot of Buttercup's fellow waterfowl, Minnie, and used it to model and print a mould for a new foot made of silicone. A later version was made that even allowed Buttercup to swim smoothly. He's no longer a lame duck!

GRECIA

Found by farmers with most of his upper beak missing, Grecia the toucan was taken to the Zoo Ave sanctuary in Costa Rica. While there, he was fitted with the **largest 3D-printed prosthetic beak**. He began singing again just a few days later!

Grecia's new 3D-printed bill measures 19 cm (7.4 in) long.

I hope I don't look a complete goose in this...

MOTALA

In 1999, an elephant named Motala lost her front left foot after stepping on a landmine. She was taken to the Hang Chat Elephant Hospital in Lampang, Thailand, where more than 30 people worked together to operate – the **most vets involved in one procedure**. But that's not the only record connected to Motala: she was later fitted with the **largest prosthetic limb**, capable of bearing 3–5 tonnes (6,600–11,000 lb).

FREDDY

When this tortoise's shell was badly damaged in a bush fire in Brazil, the "Animal Avengers" came to the rescue. Made up of four vets, a dental surgeon and a 3D designer, the group printed a new plastic shell (below) for Freddy, then painted it to resemble the original (right).

Motala had to be re-fitted with new prosthetic legs as she grew bigger.

MEET THE SUPERVET

NO WAY!

Noel founded a music concert called ONE LIVE!

Professor Noel Fitzpatrick, aka "The Supervet", has been pioneering new ways of treating animals – both in and out of the surgery – for years. Here, he tells us what drew him to a career as a vet and how he envisages the future of medicine.

Did you consider any other jobs when growing up?

I knew from an early age, growing up on the family farm in Ireland, that I wanted to become a vet. My best friends were animals and I was determined to study hard so that one day I could be good enough. Of course, that's a moving target most days, and often I still don't feel "good enough", because biology will always humble you – no matter how good you think you are!

How has technology shaped your veterinary work?

I was very frustrated by the lack of options available for my patients. I realized that I could either spend my career feeling powerless or I could do something to change that. I think it's very important that we embrace the technological revolution in medicine.

However, in veterinary medicine as in human medicine, there is a moral imperative to consider in every case what the right thing to do might be. For example, performing a total joint replacement on a very old dog may not be in their best interest. Just because it's possible to do something, it doesn't make it the right thing to do. The quality of life of each individual patient is the number-one consideration.

Which of your surgical feats are you most proud of?

I don't really get proud because my mum always said, "Pride takes a fall." I can do the same operation on two consecutive days with the same amount of effort and either succeed or fail.

Thanks to the dedication of the team of clinical and engineering colleagues I work with, we have conceived and developed several world firsts, including total joint reconstructions, 3D-printed custom

Noel hanging out with his own dog, border terrier Keira.

joint replacements, limb salvage prostheses, limb deformity correction, plus spinal disc replacement and fusion options.

Noel with a patient who required treatment for a limb deformity.

How do you strike a balance between engaging with your patients and not getting too emotionally invested?
All I ever wanted to do was to be an advocate for the animals, and I don't think that surgeons should be detached from their emotions and from being fully invested in the outcome of each and every patient.

Our vocation is to give animals hope and to provide quality of life in the best way possible. There are some cases where I become quite emotional because of the journey we've been on or because of failure along the way. I think it's very important that society understands that this is surgery on a biological organism – it's not putting an exhaust on a car. Therefore, there are no guarantees and I would caution society to try not to lash out and be angry when things don't go well. The most emotionally challenging part of my job is dealing with the pain of failure, especially when families hold you responsible when in fact you have done all that you can to save life and limb. I try to focus on all of the animals we have saved through innovation whenever I'm feeling sad.

Tell us about The Humanimal Trust.
I founded The Humanimal Trust to champion a united advancement of animal and human health care. It promotes and supports the message of "One Medicine" that will integrate the developments in veterinary and medical science and education. It will build closer working relationships between doctors and vets, so everyone benefits.

It's crazy in my view that the medical advances that animals facilitate for humans rarely come back to help the animals themselves. This will continue unless we all adopt a new thought process.

Ultimately, The Humanimal Trust will be a platform for good in the world, such that human and animal medicine will move forward together.

Any tips for readers hoping to become a vet?
What matters is that you care! I personally feel that it's a real shame that there isn't a test for the size of your heart, as I think that compassion, empathy and love are way more important in a vet than brains. You need enough ego to believe in yourself, but you need to be able to leave it at the door and genuinely want to be an advocate for the animal. If you believe in yourself, work very, very hard, because everybody has the potential for greatness and nobody has the right to rob you of your dream.

For the full interview with Professor Noel Fitzpatrick, go to www. guinnessworldrecords. com/2018.

Oscar tests out his new bionic paws after a three-hour op.

In 2009, Noel performed a groundbreaking operation on Oscar the cat (top). The misfortunate moggy had a nasty encounter with farming machinery in Jersey, UK, leading to the loss of his back feet. To put a spring back in his step, Supervet fitted a pair of brand-new metal paws. Oscar is the **first animal to receive two bionic leg implants**; Noel proudly keeps his official GWR certificate in the office at his Surrey-based practice.

FUR-THER INFO

Professor Fitzpatrick is a busy man! He has run the Fitzpatrick Referrals veterinary practice since 2005: **fitzpatrickreferrals.co.uk**. British TV series *The Supervet*, which follows the stories of some of the surgery's patients, was on its ninth series as of 2017. On top of all that, Noel is also the founder of The Humanimal Trust, which campaigns for greater collaboration between animal and human medicine practitioners.

Noel "scrubbed up" during surgery at Fitzpatrick Referrals.

UP, UP AND AWAY!

Who needs wings when you can fly by helicopter? You wouldn't usually expect to see these animals in the sky, but rescue missions have taken them to new heights!

FAST FACT

Rhinos are hunted for their horns, a practice that has brought them close to extinction. From the 1960s to the 1990s, the black rhino population in Africa shrank from around 65,000 to just 2,000.

BLACK RHINO

Pigs might fly... but rhinos really *are* flying in South Africa, up to 1,000 m (3,280 ft) high! Critically endangered, the thick-skinned animals are being transferred to safer habitats by the Black Rhino Range Expansion Project. Airlifting is better for the health of these hefty beasts than travelling by land: it's smoother and faster, reducing the amount of time they need to be sedated. Before the rhinos are let loose again, their horns are fitted with radio transmitters so their whereabouts can be monitored.

MAMMOTH

The Jarkov mammoth is named after the nine-year-old boy who found the frozen beast in Siberia back in 1997. It's thought to have been alive around 23,000 years ago, making it one of the oldest intact mammoths ever discovered. Trapped in a block of mud and ice (right), it was lifted by helicopter to defrost in a cave, where scientists can now study this real Ice Age giant.

COW

Holy cow! Who knows what this injured bovine might have been thinking as it soared over the Swiss Alps to visit the vet? Unable to walk down the mountain owing to a hurt hoof, the animal was finally *moo*-vable once in a harnessed sling, suspended from a helicopter.

NO WAY!

It took at least an hour to clean each penguin by hand!

AFRICAN PENGUINS

Penguins may not be able to fly naturally, but the **largest airlift of penguins** took place in 2000. Between 15,000 and 20,000 African penguins were rescued after an oil spill north of Cape Town, South Africa. Oil damages the birds' natural waterproofing, leaving them cold and unable to swim for food. Nearly all of the penguins recovered and were set free in clean water farther up the coast (top).

POLAR BEARS

The Canadian town of Churchill in Manitoba isn't known as the "polar bear capital" for nothing! When bears become too curious and cause trouble for the locals, they are held in a special compound, checked over, then flown north for release, far out of harm's way. The tranquillized animals are airlifted in nets, sometimes two or three at a time (see right). Being the world's **largest bears** – with adult males typically weighing some 400–600 kg (880–1,320 lb) – they make for heavyweight cargo!

I *told* him that we'd get caught!

NATURAL-BORN SURVIVORS

There are some incredible stories out there of "miracle" animals pulling through extraordinary situations. Here are some of the hardiest, who defied the odds to live another day...

In Dec 1999, after an earthquake struck Chinese Taipei, a cat was found in the rubble of a collapsed building... 80 days later! Dehydrated, starving and barely breathing, the frail feline was rushed to a veterinary hospital, where it made a full recovery. This was the **longest survival by a trapped cat post-earthquake**.

Phew! I made it by a whisker...

FAST FACT

The quake-surviving cat weighed less than 2 kg (4 lb 6.5 oz) when it was found – half the weight of a healthy cat of its size. Demolition workers who thought it was dead were stopped from throwing the animal in the rubbish!

Dosha was shot below one eye and then later suffered from hypothermia.

They say that *cats* have nine lives, but a dog called Dosha has had her fair share of luck, too. Hit by a car near her home in California, USA, she was then shot by a police officer to put her out of pain. Presumed dead, she was placed in a dog-pound freezer, before being discovered sitting up, alive two hours later! She holds the record for **most "fatal" incidents survived by a dog in one day**.

Lillie the black Labrador holds the record for **longest time trapped by a dog**. She was missing from her home in New Hampshire, USA, for 49 days before being found at the bottom of a 1.5-m (5-ft) well. It was just lucky for Lillie that a passer-by heard her barking!

It's still a mystery how a young dog called Kyle swallowed a 15-in (38.1-cm) bread knife. It was only discovered in the puppy's stomach after an X-ray. The serrated blade – the **longest solid object swallowed by a dog** – had to be surgically removed.

It could be straight out of *Finding Dory*... At Shima Marineland in Japan, a live goldfish was thrown into a tank as food for bigger fish. The slippery swimmer escaped through a tiny gap into a filtration unit, where it fed on scraps that passed through. It lived there undiscovered for seven years!

When a tuna boat exploded and sank off the coast of Oregon, USA, in 2013, there were two cats on board. Both Topaz and Jasper swam to join their owners on the rescue boat – though Jasper clung to the bow for as long as possible before taking the plunge!

Despite having his head chopped off, a chicken named Mike went on to survive for 18 months! The fowl was taken on tour round the USA in 1945, being fed water and liquid food through a dropper, before departing this life finally in Arizona. He gets the record for **longest-surviving headless chicken**.

In 1978, Alex Maclennan found a ewe still alive after 50 days stuck in a snowdrift in Sutherland, UK. It's believed that the sheep's hot breath created air holes in the snow, helping it to achieve the **longest survival by a buried sheep**.

Miracle Mike was able to survive so long owing to part of his brain stem remaining intact!

A DAY AT THE PET SHELTER

With over 150 years' experience rehoming animals, the world-famous Battersea Dogs & Cats Home was the ideal place to learn all about what goes on at a pet shelter. The hardest bit was resisting taking home a new furry friend!

Battersea Dogs & Cats Home in London, UK, has been in its current location since 1871. This centre had been operating for 145 years 312 days as of 21 March 2017, making it the **longest-running pet shelter on the same site**. Here, GWR's Editor-in-Chief, Craig Glenday, presents a certificate to Veterinary Director, Shaun Opperman, and Head of Canine Behaviour, Ali Taylor, who were giving us a tour. Ali revealed: "Battersea is constantly changing... it's not just about rescuing and rehoming – there's a lot more work that goes on behind the scenes!"

NO WAY!

Battersea has cared for some 3.1 million dogs and cats!

A historical shot of Battersea Dogs & Cats Home when the shelter was a lot smaller!

On arriving at Battersea, every dog and cat gets a full health check. The first thing looked for in a stray is a microchip, to see if there is a registered owner. A vet also logs vital stats, such as heart rate and weight. During their stay, animals get regular check-ups and receive medicine and treatment such as vaccinations.

Honey the Chihuahua is given a full bill of health before being rehomed.

Battersea started taking in cats in 1883. For the first time in the rescue centre's history, more cats were rehomed than dogs in 2015. Cattery Team Leader Rosa Steele (right) says that, on average, they receive about six new cats per day!

Please do not touch the cats through door gaps as this spreads cat flu

The cattery is a bit like a hotel, with glass "pods" and soothing classical music!

Volunteer Barbara plays with Ale the greyhound in one of the indoor exercise runs.

Rosa spends some cuddle time with Batman the cat.

TO COMMEMORATE THE OPENING OF THE MARY TEALBY KENNELS BY HER MAJESTY THE QUEEN 17 MARCH 2015 WHERE LIFE BEGINS

Volunteers play a big role in caring for the 7,000 or so animals that arrive at Battersea each year. Hundreds of people donate their time to assist with everyday tasks, such as cleaning the kennels, feeding and spending time with the residents so that they don't get lonely.

Battersea Dogs & Cats Home even has a Royal Patron! Former Patron Queen Elizabeth II visited the shelter in 2015 to officially open a new kennel block (above). The kennels are named after Mary Tealby, who founded the organization back in 1860. As of 2017, Battersea's Royal Patron is Camilla, the Duchess of Cornwall.

Dogs can stretch their legs in the on-site paddocks. These astroturf areas are filled with toys and agility equipment, so Battersea hounds can do some fun training exercises. When we visited, the shelter was close to completing a doggie swimming pool, too!

FUR-THER INFO

Since Battersea Dogs & Cats Home welcomed its first stray dog in 1860 (they moved to their current site in 1871), it has been placing animals at the centre of everything it does. The rescue centre is still working hard to achieve its vision that every dog and cat should live in a home where it is treated with love and respect. For more information, visit **www.battersea.org.uk**, or go to p.211.

BATTERSEA DOGS & CATS HOME

Former Battersea resident Squirt now represents the charity at special events.

LEAP DOG

Border collie Neo never "tyres" of jumping around! As his recent TV appearance in *Secret Life of Dogs* showed, he's happiest when tackling slaloms or pouncing to incredible heights. Read more about Neo's amazing skills, and other stunt-pulling pooches, on the next page.

TRICKS & STUNTS

TOP DOGS

Your pooch might be able to sit up and beg, roll over or high five... but these stunt-pulling pups are in a league of their own. Treats all round for these clever canines!

JESSICA

Jack Russell terrier Jessica teamed up with her owner, Rachael Grylls, to achieve the **most skips by a person and dog on the same rope in one minute**. The bouncy pair completed 59 jumps on 1 Dec 2016.

PURIN

Goalie gosh! Purin the beagle from Japan is one sporty hound. "Saving" 14 shots at goal, she broke her own record for **most balls caught in one minute by a dog** in 2015.

SUPER WAN WAN CIRCUS

Since the 1950s, Japan's Super Wan Wan Circus has been rescuing and training abandoned dogs. Taught by their handler Uchida Geinousha (below left), the prancing pooches jumped their way to the record for **most dogs skipping on the same rope**: 14!

Mayonnaise the poodle kicked off the canine troupe's skipping craze.

DING DING

Travelling upright on two legs might seem like a *tall order for a dog* – but for Ding Ding from China, it's a walk in the park... Taking the record off Jiffpom (see pp.84–85), the poodle achieved the **fastest 10 m on hind legs by a dog** on 23 Jun 2016, speeding along in just 4.99 sec. Ding Ding's owner has also trained him how to catch Frisbees and collect coins.

Ding Ding has a rather colourful wardrobe of canine clothes too!

Neo's agility skills have earned him the nickname of the "parkour collie".

Well, I did say I'd jump through hoops to get extra treats at dinner time...

NEO

Working dogs by tradition, border collies such as Neo have plenty of energy! Having a professional trainer for an owner helps put that to good use. Steve Bailey knew exactly how to keep his pet happy, channelling Neo's liveliness into coordinated slaloms and jumps. The training paid off when he achieved the **fastest 10-hoop slalom by a dog** – 8.58 sec – on 27 Jul 2016.

Jumping through hoops isn't Neo's only party trick. He's also mastered the art of "wall running". This manoeuvre involves jumping onto a vertical surface and running several steps with all four feet making contact with the wall. Who said dogs can't defy gravity?

SUPER-DOG

SMURF

MEET SMURF, WHO HOLDS THE RECORD FOR **MOST TRICKS PERFORMED BY A DOG IN ONE MINUTE.** THE PARSON RUSSELL TERRIER MANAGED AN AMAZING 32 STUNTS! WHEN HE'S NOT BREAKING RECORDS OR APPEARING ON TV, SMURF HELPS AROUND THE HOUSE: HE CAN MAKE THE BED, LOAD THE WASHING MACHINE AND FETCH A DRINK FROM THE FRIDGE!

SARAH HUMPHREYS

SMURF LIVES WITH HIS OWNER AND TRAINER, SARAH, IN HERTFORDSHIRE, UK. THEY HAVE BEEN TOGETHER SINCE SMURF WAS 14 WEEKS OLD, WHEN HIS ABILITIES QUICKLY BECAME APPARENT. WITH SARAH'S HELP, HE RECEIVED A PALM DOG AWARD AT CANNES FOR HIS ROLE IN THE FILM SIGHTSEERS (2012). HE ALSO WON TV TALENT SHOW SUPERSTAR DOGS IN 2014.

Mid-roll-over, Smurf kindly played dead for the cameras!

SARAH PUT SMURF THROUGH HIS PACES TO ACHIEVE THE RECORD. THE SPEEDILY PERFORMED TRICKS INCLUDED ROLLING OVER (ABOVE RIGHT), "SPEAKING" (RIGHT), JUMPING OVER HER ARM (FAR RIGHT), WALKING ON HIND LEGS, LIMPING, REVERSING THROUGH SARAH'S LEGS AND DOING A PAW-STAND AGAINST THE WALL!

SUPER-CAT

DIDGA

YOU MAY HAVE ALREADY SEEN DIDGA – SHORT FOR DIDGERIDOO – SHOWING OFF HER SKATEBOARDING SKILLS ON P.57. BUT THE ROLLING RESCUE KITTY ALSO SET THE RECORD FOR **MOST TRICKS PERFORMED BY A CAT IN ONE MINUTE**: 24! SHE'S ONE MULTI-TALENTED MOGGIE!

ROBERT DOLLWET

DIDGA'S OWNER, ROBERT, WAS A DOG TRAINER FOR MANY YEARS. NOW HE CALLS HIMSELF "CATMANTOO"! HE FOUND DIDGA AT A SHELTER NEAR HIS HOME IN NEW SOUTH WALES, AUSTRALIA. HER FAVOURITE FOOD IS KANGAROO MINCE – THE KEY TO ENCOURAGING DIDGA TO FIRST STEP ON A SKATEBOARD AS A KITTEN!

After jumping into Robert's hands, Didga is able to balance on just one of his palms!

THE TRICKS DIDGA PERFORMED FOR HER RECORD INCLUDED ROLLING OVER (ABOVE LEFT), HIGH-FIVING (FAR LEFT), JUMPING ON TO ROBERT'S HANDS (LEFT), SPINNING ON THE SPOT, WAVING HER PAW AND JUMPING OVER A BAR WHILE RIDING A SKATEBOARD – WHICH IS CALLED A "HIPPIE JUMP"!

WOOLLY JUMPERS

They've all jumped into the record books... From a leaping llama to a prancing pig, meet the bouncing beasts with a real spring in their step.

FAST FACT

Llamas are native to South America, and have been used for centuries in the Andes as pack animals. Although they're related to camels, they don't have a hump.

CASPA

Caspa the llama is a "total diva" according to his owner, Sue Williams (inset left). But then he would be: at the 2015 DogFest show in Cheshire, UK, he achieved the **highest bar jump by a llama**, clearing 1.13 m (3 ft 8.5 in). Caspa is now a star among his show-jumping pals at the Blackrock Llama Centre in Wales. But he had some teething problems when he first arrived, showing his dislike for humans by spitting, kicking and biting! He finally found his feet – or hooves – after Sue put him through agility training.

LOL

HOW DO HEDGEHOGS PLAY LEAPFROG?

VERY CAREFULLY!

KOTETSU

The **highest jump by a pig** is 70 cm (2 ft 3.5 in). This huge leap for porcine kind was achieved by Kotetsu, a pot-bellied pig at the Mokumoku Tedsukuri Farm in Japan.

Pot-bellied pigs originated in Vietnam, and are often kept as pets.

Is it a bird?... Is it a plane?... No, it's supercat!

ALLEY

Look at this moggy move! It's Alley achieving the **longest jump by a cat** – 6 ft (182.8 cm) – in Austin, Texas, USA. The pouncing puss got her name after being rescued from an alley in Chicago, USA. She is now a member of the Amazing Acro-Cats circus troupe, founded by Alley's owner, Samantha Martin.

A red kangaroo holds the record for the **longest jump by a kangaroo**. It occurred during a chase in New South Wales, Australia, in 1951, when a female covered 12.8 m (42 ft) in one leap.

en Cindy clears a bar, she's rewarded with her favourite game: Frisbee.

CINDERELLA MAY

A greyhound named Cinderella May a Holly Grey holds the record for the **highest jump by a dog**. She cleared 172.7 cm (5 ft 8 in) at the Purina Incredible Dog Challenge National Finals in Missouri, USA. No wonder the rescue dog has earned the nickname "Soaring Cindy"!

A puma, also known as a mountain lion, holds the record for **highest jump by a mammal**. The momentous leap was 7 m (23 ft) straight up in the air from standstill.

LAMBORGHINI

A sheep called *Lamb*orghini? He'd better be fast! Luckily, the Friesland/Dorset Down cross holds the record for **most races won by a sheep** – 165 out of 179 season races. The 250-m (820-ft) track races at Odds Farm Park near High Wycombe, UK, include hurdles and hairpin bends. Here he is (#4) carrying his regular "jockey" – a soft-toy pig named Del Trotter. *Baaaaa*-rilliant!

The common froghopper can make the **highest jump by an insect**: 70 cm (27.5 in). When it launches, the insect accelerates at 4,000 m (13,123 ft) per sec and overcomes a g-force of more than 400 times its own body weight!

PALANCING ACTS

When records and global glory are in the balance, the pressure is always on... But that didn't trouble these cool customers. Keeping a level head, they steadied their nerves and didn't let their resolve wobble once!

OZZY

Sure-footed Osbert Humperdinck Pumpernickle, aka Ozzy, must have got some funny looks when he took up the hobby of tightrope-walking. The border collie-kelpie cross had to train for many weeks – along with his owner Nick Johnson (UK) – but it paid off. In 2013, he walked away with the world record title for **fastest time to cross a tightrope by a dog**, covering 3.5 m (11 ft 5 in) in a lightning-quick 18.22 sec.

NO WAY!

Ozzy can also balance on a rope on just two paws!

QUICK QUIZ

Q. WHAT IS THE TECHNICAL NAME FOR TIGHTROPE-WALKING?

A. FUNAMBULISM

PURIN

Purin the beagle from Japan is on a roll when it comes to breaking records, with three achieved to date! The first record she set was the **fastest 10 m travelled on a ball by a dog** (left). She did it in 11.90 sec in 2015, but on 7 Apr 2017 she surpassed herself with a time of 9.45 sec.

You can see more of Purin's skills in action on pp.110–11!

The heat is really on with this one!

NATURE'S STEADY EDDIES

HARLSO

They don't come any more level-headed than Harley the Balancing Hound, aka Harlso. The sausage dog from Belfast, Northern Ireland, UK, became a huge hit after pictures of his trademark trick were posted online. His skill for keeping still was first discovered by accident when his owner set a toy chicken on his head and Harlso managed to keep it there for two minutes!

FAST FACT

Harlso has been sent many objects to try to balance from his thousands of fans. The dachshund has even inspired other pets to get in on the balancing act, with owners sharing snaps of their pets defying gravity.

The ring-tailed lemur from Madagascar uses its bushy tail as a balancing aid when jumping between trees. It's also used as a form of communication among lemurs.

On thin branches and vines, gibbons walk on their back legs and use their long arms to balance – just like human tightrope-walkers!

GAIGAI WUWU

Another pet that has taken the internet by storm thanks to his amazing balancing skills is Gaigai Wuwu, a cool-as-a-cucumber cat from Malaysia. His paws have supported everything from food to books – and even playing cards!

Goats don't grow on trees, but they're great at climbing them! In Morocco, they perch on the branches of argan trees to feast on the delicious fruit.

THE ELEPHANT ORCHESTRA

I wonder if *Ellie* Goulding needs a support act...?

Since 1997, the Thai Elephant Conservation Center in Lampang, Thailand, has been home to a group of mammoth musicians. The jumbo stars, retired from logging work, have a real ear for music and are known as the Thai Elephant Orchestra (TEO).

Working elephants have a close bond with their "mahout" (keeper). This duo are shown at a recording session in 2006. The big performers often improvise their own music, only lightly directed by mahouts.

Consisting of up to 16 members, TEO is the **largest animal orchestra**. It was founded by scientist and composer Dave Soldier and "Professor Elephant" Richard Lair, who set up the centre. Dave built giant traditional instruments that could be played with either a trunk or a stick. After demonstrating how the instruments worked, he let the elephants take the lead.

Dave Soldier firmly believes that elephants enjoy making music for music's sake, just like us.

Dave Soldier (right) is convinced elephants have a musical ear. He once played an off-key note on a "ranat" (Thai xylophone) and the elephants then avoided the instrument. TEO mainly uses the five notes of a Thai musical scale.

Luuk Kob is a former drummer for the Thai Elephant Orchestra. While music is his first love, it isn't the only string to his bow. After a little acting training, Luuk Kob was one of several elephants to appear in Disney's *Operation Dumbo Drop*. This 1995 movie is all about transporting an elephant through the Vietnamese jungle.

Richard Lair (below) is TEO's conductor. In the early days, the elephants learned the harmonica, and also took to the drums and ranat. Fittingly, the gong they play is a circular saw blade retrieved from an illegal logging operation. Local people say that the orchestra's sound is similar to Thai temple music.

FAST FACT

In 2012, a New York orchestra performed an arrangement of one of TEO's songs. When asked what they thought, most of the audience assumed that the piece was by a well-known composer!

GUINNESS WORLD RECORDS

NO WAY!

Some of TEO's elephants are also keen painters!

The elephants have starred on three CDs to date. The second album, *Elephonic Rhapsodies*, features "Phong's Solo", a song composed by Phong the elephant. It also includes a rendition of Beethoven's Symphony No.6, which TEO performed with a marching band from a local high school.

Elephonic Rhapsodies

THAI ELEPHANT ORCHESTRA

DAVE SOLDIER • RICHARD LAIR

ANIMAL ARTISTS

If you think animals can't paint, this group of creative creatures might change your mind. Some of their colourful – admittedly abstract – works have even found buyers and gallery space!

ARBOR

Rescued from the streets of Las Vegas in Nevada, USA, Arbor the painting pooch has been encouraged by her owners to express herself on canvas. Her finished works of art are then auctioned online, with the money going towards helping homeless animals – a cause close to Arbor's heart!

JONAO

A clever male sea lion named Jonao was *apeing* human calligraphers when he painted the Chinese character for "monkey" (right). Taught by his trainer, Tsutomu Kawabata, the marine mammal showed off his skilful strokes at the Sea Paradise aquarium in Yokohama, Japan.

LOL

WHICH CAT IS THE GREATEST ARTIST?

LIONARDO DA VINCI!

PIGCASSO

At four weeks old, Pigcasso the pig found herself in a slaughterhouse – but Joanne Lefson saved her bacon. With treats and a technique called clicker training – usually used for dogs – Joanne helped the sow find her artistic calling, and her name! At their home near Cape Town, South Africa, Pigcasso has learned to dip a brush into paint with her mouth and apply it to canvas. She even gives her works a unique "signature": a snout print!

I'll call this one *Straight from the Horse's Mouth...*

Cholla first became interested in brushwork when his owner was painting the paddock fence.

CHOLLA

Cholla the horse certainly has poise when painting – perhaps he caught the artistic vibe from his ballerina owner. Pictured here in his paddock in Nevada, USA, the expressive equine would choose his own brush and colour, then enjoy making marks on paper. Cholla's watercolours were even judged good enough to be exhibited by a gallery in Venice, Italy!

CAROL

For many years, an Asian elephant named Carol was a star resident at San Diego Zoo Safari Park in California, USA. Having arrived as a calf in 1968, she was befriended by the zoo's goodwill ambassador, Joan Embery. Joan enabled Carol to paint – the elephant would wrap her trunk round a brush (see below). The results were sold at zoo events, raising money for elephant conservation. Carol also made several TV appearances before she died in 2007.

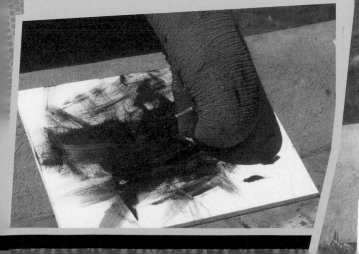

NOT JUST PRETTY POLLIES

Parrots are some of the most colourful birds in the world. But did you know they're also really intelligent? Meet the record-breaking super-parrots that prove they're anything but bird-brained!

NO WAY!

A macaw's beak can crack into a coconut!

Skipper bounced for joy after achieving her record.

SKIPPER BLUE

Hoopla! That's the name of the game here... And it resulted in Skipper Blue achieving the record for **most rings placed on a target by a parrot in one minute**. The blue-and-gold macaw hooped 19 rings in her backyard in California, USA. She was overseen by trainer Wendy Horton and GWR adjudicator Sofia Greenacre (below). Skipper set the record on Guinness World Records Day 2016.

FACTS
at your FINGERTIPS

Wild macaws have a varied diet of small mammals, reptiles, fruits and nuts – and even poisonous seeds.

The backward-facing toes on parrots' feet give them an iron grip on food and branches, but are not so great for walking.

Pet macaws need lots of attention. They show they're bored by throwing things from their cages or even pulling out their own feathers.

ZAC

Zac the harlequin macaw has *two* records to his name. His first was the **most basketball slam dunks by a parrot in one minute**: 22. Then he achieved the **most canned drinks opened by a parrot in one minute**, making 35 sodas fizz! He accomplished these feats in San José, California, USA, with his trainers Julie and Ed Cardoza. He used to take part in performances in which he'd scooter, skateboard and raise a flag. Now in his 20s, Zac has retired from shows, and now "just shoots hoops for the fun of it"!

ALEX

The **most intelligent parrot** was an African grey called Alex. Animal psychologist Irene Pepperberg worked with him for 30 years. In that time, Alex learned words for more than 35 objects and seven colours. He could converse in short sentences and also identify different shapes.

The Alex Foundation continues research into grey-parrot intelligence to this day.

BIG PICTURE

A STROKE OF GENIUS

While Bini the rabbit loves to shoot hoops, he's also a talented artist. Give him a brush, canvas and acrylic paints and he'll create a masterpiece... Just don't take the paintbrush away from him before he's finished or he'll be *hopping* mad!

GUINNESS WORLD RECORDS

BASKETBALL BUNNY

This rabbit's nose for the net has made him an internet sensation. Bini holds the record for **most slam dunks by a rabbit in one minute**, with seven. Originally born in Israel, the hoop-loving pet now lives in Los Angeles, California, USA, with his owner, Shai Asor. At first, Shai taught Bini tricks such as standing and spinning, but when he found the bouncy bunny playing with a ball one day, he set him up with his very own basketball court!

FAST FACT

Bini is a Holand Lop, which is a dwarf breed. But that hasn't stopped him from being a high achiever. He has millions of social media followers online! even sells his artwork online!

CAT IQ TEST

Cats are often thought to be less intelligent than dogs. But there's plenty of evidence to suggest that they have as much brain power – they're just less eager to please! How clever is *your* kitty? See how it gets on with these tests...

LEARNING TEST

Teach your cat to turn in a circle by moving some food or a toy 360° above it. For the first five tries, give your cat the food or a chance to play with the toy after half a circle. For the next five tries, reward after a full circle. Now repeat but with no incentive – just indicate a circle with your hand.

1 Your cat turns in a full circle (i.e., 360°) just by interpreting your hand gesture.

2 Your cat turns, but doesn't make a full circle. It might need a few more tries with a treat.

3 Your cat makes no attempt to turn. Try again with tastier food or a more exciting toy.

Tracking is an important skill for cats, who hunt small animals that dart in and out of sight.

OBSERVATIONAL TEST

Upturn two cups and, while your cat is watching, place a treat under one. Slowly switch the positions of the cups and let your cat approach them. Which cup does it head for?

1 The cup with the treat. Your cat can follow the location of food even when it can no longer see it. Useful for hunting mice!

2 The cup without the treat. Your cat is unable to follow the location of food when it can no longer see it. Keep practising!

3 Neither. The treat might not have been enticing enough for the cat to try to track where it went. Find something tastier?

FAST FACT

Cats have nearly twice the number of neurons in their cerebral cortex – the part of the brain responsible for intelligence – than dogs do. Some studies suggest they also have longer-lasting memories.

FUR-THER INFO

international **cat care**

This cat IQ test was compiled by Dr Sarah Ellis, a feline behaviour expert for International Cat Care (ICC). The charity aims to engage, educate and empower people to improve the health and welfare of cats by sharing advice and training. You can access free information to help you look after your cat at **www.icatcare.org**.

QUANTITY TEST

When your cat is hungry, offer it two saucers, both with the same food on it that it likes, e.g., cooked chicken or fish. One portion should be at least half the size of the other. Which saucer does the cat go to first?

1 The big portion. Your cat can tell the difference between small and large, and knows that bigger is better!

2 The small portion. Your cat may not be able to tell the difference in size, or simply wasn't very hungry.

3 Your cat didn't go for either. Perhaps it wasn't hungry enough? Try again when it has more of an appetite!

Cats will often purr in anticipation of food – or simply when content!

RECOGNITION TEST

On a phone, record four different people calling your cat's name: three of your friends first, then one family member who lives with your cat. Get someone to play the recordings from outside the room while you watch your cat's responses.

1 Your cat showed more interest in the call when it was a family member. It seems to recognize familiar voices.

2 It reacted the same way to all the recordings. Your cat is clearly attuned to its name, but maybe not specific voices.

3 Your cat didn't pay any attention to the recordings at all. Perhaps it can't hear them – try upping the volume.

You might need to attach a speaker to your phone to boost the volume.

MEMORY TEST

Place four little pots/bowls in different places in a room. When your cat is hungry, let it watch you place a cat biscuit in each pot. After it has eaten from two, remove your cat from the room for 30 sec. Then let it back into the room.

1 Your cat goes straight to the pots with the uneaten food. It remembers which it has already eaten from.

2 Your cat goes to the pots it has eaten from. It recalls the game but seems to have forgotten where it has already been.

3 Your cat does not go to any of the pots. It may not remember where they are, or is simply not motivated to eat.

Repeat the experiment and try hiding the pots in different places.

HOW SMART IS YOUR CAT?

Mostly 1s: Your puss is a genius! If it were human it would be a member of Mensa.
Mostly 2s: Your cat is doing well. Keep going using treats and toys and your moggy may get even smarter.
Mostly 3s: Cats often prefer doing their own thing. Try again another day to see if you get a different result!

DOG IQ TEST

Some dogs are endearingly dim, while others show a high level of canine cunning. Put your pooch through its paces and see how well it does here... Who said you can't teach an old dog new tricks?

LEARNING TEST

A dog can learn to associate the word "sit" with the act of sitting. It might learn that sitting results in a tasty treat or a toy. But does your dog actually understand the word "sit", or is it reacting to something else? Ask your dog to sit using just your voice (e.g., no hand gestures). What does it do?

1 Sits straight away. A star pupil – your dog can associate the verbal "sit" command with the act of sitting.

2 Performs a different trick. Your dog knows you want it to do something, but hasn't grasped exactly what yet.

3 Wanders off or looks blank. It might not understand without a hand gesture to reinforce the verbal instruction.

Sitting when asked is a type of canine learning called "operant conditioning".

Research suggests that dogs inherited an ability to count from wolves.

COUNTING TEST

Place two non-transparent bowls on the floor, some distance apart. Keep your dog far enough away that it can't see into the bowls. Make sure it watches as you drop, one at a time, six treats into one bowl, two into the other. Then ask your dog to choose. Repeat, changing which bowl you fill with more treats.

1 Your dog goes straight to the bowl with the most treats, every time. This might mean that your clever canine can count!

2 Your dog goes to the same bowl each time, no matter how many treats it contains. It's not so fussy – any food will do!

3 Your dog goes to the bowl with fewer treats each time, or shows no obvious preference. No counting going on.

FAST FACT

Border collies have come top in studies aiming to find the brightest dog breed. One collie in the USA, called Chaser, learned the names of more than 1,000 objects and could retrieve each by verbal command.

FUR-THER INFO

This IQ test was compiled by animal behaviourist Rosie Barclay, chair of the Association of Pet Behaviour Counsellors. APBC is a network of qualified counsellors based mainly in the UK. They work on referral from veterinary surgeons to treat behaviour problems in dogs, cats, birds, rabbits, horses and other pets. Visit **apbc.org.uk**.

APBC
ASSOCIATION OF PET
BEHAVIOUR COUNSELLORS

IMITATION TEST

With your dog watching, place a biscuit at the far end of a piece of paper and push the paper under a sofa/bed that the dog can't get under. The empty end of the sheet should be sticking out. Show how to retrieve the biscuit a couple of times by sliding out the paper. Now, let your dog try...

1 Your dog immediately pulls the paper to retrieve the biscuit. This smart pup is clearly a pro "copycat".

2 Your dog looks at you for assistance. Judging the task too difficult, it expects you to help out.

3 Your dog paws at the paper a lot, eventually getting the biscuit out by scrabbling. It's more luck than judgement.

Dogs have learned to look to their owners for help if they find themselves in a difficult situation.

MEMORY TEST

Pick an old toy whose name your dog knows well. Add a toy whose name your dog has not learned. Ask the dog to fetch the toy he knows. Then ask it to fetch the other toy, giving it an unfamiliar name. What does your dog do?

1 Collects the new toy and brings it back. Your dog recalls names and seems to have used the process of elimination!

2 Retrieves the old toy. Your dog has learned what a toy is and to bring it to you, but not the difference between names.

3 Moves towards the toys but doesn't bring anything back. It may not understand. Try different toys.

Dogs seem to be able to follow any pointing gesture. Try pointing with your foot or elbow.

OBSERVATIONAL TEST

Place a treat under one of two upturned cups so that your dog can see but not touch. After 10 sec, point to the cup without a treat and let the dog investigate. Repeat three times but change the cup you put the treat under. Is your dog clever enough to ignore your deceptive pointing?

1 Your dog goes straight to the cup that contains the treat, ignoring the cup that you're pointing to. There's no fooling this sharp-eyed pooch!

2 Your dog goes to the cup you pointed to. What a faithful fido! See what happens if you nod your head towards the empty cup instead.

3 Your dog doesn't investigate either cup. It may not recall there are treats hidden, or yet know what pointing means.

HOW SMART IS YOUR DOG?

Mostly 1s: Your pooch is a canine Einstein! You and your dog have great communication skills.
Mostly 2s: You're doing really well – keep training using those rewards and your dog will get the knack.
Mostly 3s: Not all dogs can – or want to – be top of the class, but all training is valuable bonding time.

TRICKS & STUNTS

READ YOUR PET'S MIND

Dogs have the same kind of chemistry that regulates our emotions, so they may experience something similar to how we feel when happy or sad. Use our exclusive guide to see what your dog's body language and behaviour can tell you about its mood...

DOGS

FRUSTRATED

Do you get upset when you can't do something – such as work out how to complete a level in a videogame? Dogs can feel like this when, for instance, they don't understand a trick you're trying to teach them; or maybe a ball they were playing with has rolled under the sofa. You can tell if Fido's feeling frustrated: he might stiffen and shake his body, lift up a paw, lick his lips, yawn and sneeze.

SCARED

Dogs can feel scared when something threatens them, such as a loud bang, being shouted at or being chased. Their hearts will beat faster, they might shiver and they may try to run away. You'll know if a dog is frightened as it will tuck its tail between its legs, its ears will flatten against its head and it will make itself look as small as possible. If it can't escape, it may react by growling, barking or biting (see below).

ANGRY

Sometimes the feelings of fear or frustration become overwhelming, turning into anger. A dog might react by growling, barking or snapping. If your pooch shows its teeth, if you can hear it growling, it goes to snap or you can see the whites of its eyes, then you can be sure it's mad! Stop whatever you're doing and slowly move away. Next time, do something your dog finds fun, easy and rewarding.

GRRR...

HAPPY

You know that feeling just before Christmas when you're super-excited and can't wait to open your presents? Dogs probably feel something similar when you're about to take them for a walk or throw a ball, or if they've found an interesting scent to follow. A dog shows happiness by wagging its tail in a fast, sweeping motion. Its mouth will be open and relaxed, often with the tongue hanging out.

CATS

Cats are notoriously cool customers, and don't have the same range of feelings we have. For example, they don't get guilty or jealous like us. However, there are some emotions we know cats *do* experience. Here's how to tell what your kitty is *feline*...

GUINNESS WORLD RECORDS

QUICK QUIZ

Q. WHAT DO YOU CALL THE HAIRS THAT STAND UP ON THE BACK OF A CAT'S NECK WHEN IT'S SCARED?

A. HACKLES

MEOW!

FRUSTRATED

Cats feel frustrated when they can't get something they want immediately – for example, if their food is taking too long to prepare, or a tasty bird is out of reach! Not getting something it anticipated will also make a cat frustrated: if its cat flap has been unexpectedly locked, for instance. A frustrated cat will have its ears rotated, its skin may ripple or twitch and its tail may thrash or thump. It will also meow loudly and persistently!

CONTENT

Cats will feel content when all their needs are met – e.g., they're not hungry or thirsty and they're comfortable. They're also happier without competition from other animals for food or attention. A cat that feels relaxed will show this by lying down, perhaps with its belly exposed, eyes closed or half closed and tail held loosely against the body. Grooming and purring are always good signs!

PURR...

SCARED

Most cats will show fear when, for instance, they meet a threatening dog. In such a case, their tail will be held low and tight against the body, ears will be flattened against the side of their head, and the head will often be held lower than the body. Their fur may stand up on end and their eyes will be open wide. Possible reactions are running away, hiding, scratching, staying very still and not eating or drinking.

SEEKING

A cat feels eager and inquisitive when it is looking for something positive – for example, food, attention or playthings. Its ears will be positioned forwards, its eyes will be alert and its tail will be held up or loosely away from the body. In this mood, a cat is likely to hunt, play, ask for attention – e.g., by rubbing against your legs – and explore its surroundings. A seeking cat might also purr in a high pitch.

CHEEKY CHIPMUNK

Nature photography can be both artistic and serious, but it can also be *really* funny! This chomping chipmunk enjoying some corn was snapped by Canadian conservationist and wildlife photographer Barb D'Arpino. It was shortlisted as a finalist in 2016's Comedy Wildlife Photography Awards, which showcases the best shots of animals doing the funniest things. Discover who else made the cut at the latest awards, and which photographer came out on top, on pp.146–47.

BEST IN SHOW 1

WORLD'S UGLIEST DOGS

While there may not be an official record for "ugliest dog", California's Sonoma-Marin Fair runs a hotly contested competition each year. The much-loved pets that enter prove that it is what's on the inside that counts. Here are some of 2016's "best lookers"!

Chinese crested Rue is partially sighted and missing a few teeth. But that doesn't stop her "borrowing" things from her family. Her owners often find socks, toys and Barbies hidden in her bed!

Rue had her eye on first prize, but had to settle for third place.

Himisaboo's hair has been likened to US President Donald Trump's!

This was the fourth time that Himisaboo had applied to be the World's Ugliest Dog. The hound's heritage is uncertain, being half-dachshund and either half-Chinese crested or half-Mexican hairless. Despite going all out in 2016 – even getting his nails done (right) – it wasn't enough to take the title. His sister Rooby Roux, however, did receive the "Spirit Award" for services to the community.

You should see me on a bad hair day!

Rascal Deux is one of a long line to embrace the ugly. Not only was his dad, Rascal, named the World's Ugliest Dog in 2002, but his great-grandpa, Chi-Chi, earned a record for his unique looks (see right).

UGLY HALL OF FAME

The all-time undisputed champion is Chi-Chi. With seven victories between 1978 and 1991, he had the **most wins of the World's Ugliest Dog contest**.

Proving that true beauty lies on the inside is Scamp. Rescued from a shelter, he is now giving back to his community. As well as working with first-graders at schools, he visits patients with Alzheimer's to brighten their day.

The highest he has ever been placed in this contest is third. Sorry, Scamp, you're just too cute for this dog-eat-dog competition!

Nana took the top spot four times in a row between 1998 and 2001. Her owner described her as a "Canardly" – as in "You can 'ardly tell her pedigree"!

Chinese crested Sweepee Rambo prevailed over 15 rivals to be declared 2016's champion. In reaching their decision, the judges considered many factors, including scruffiness and even smell! The 17-year-old Sweepee, who often wears a diaper, was the runaway winner. Her owner Jason describes her as a "ride or die chick" because she loves to join him on his motorcycle.

Three hounds have been crowned ugliest of them all on three occasions to date: Li'l Sam (2003–05; pictured), Mai Tai (1994–95, 1997) and Lady Pink (1990, 1992–93).

FURRY FASHIONISTAS

Who says catwalks can't also be for dogs? Here, groomed to perfection and dressed to impress are some of the world's most fashionable fidos and more...

These fluorescent-tinted pooches showcase the canine art of Californian dog groomer Catherine "Cat" Opson. Cat uses pet-friendly dyes to colour her miniature poodles' fur. Porsche (right and below) dazzles with a blue rinse, red highlights and a rainbow coat. Meanwhile Kobe's look (bottom and bottom right) was inspired by *Sesame Street*: dyed and sculpted into the poodle's coat are portraits of some of the show's best-known characters, including Bert, Ernie and Elmo.

Okay, darling, I'm ready for my close-up...

Cat even included Ernie's "Rubber Duckie", shaping it from Kobe's tail.

HAIRY HEROES!

Great Danes (from left) Gabe, Ella and Pandora watch the action in St Louis, USA.

Did you know that doggy dress-up even has the potential to break records? In 2012, Nestlé Purina PetCare achieved the **most dogs in costumed attire**: 1,326 (above). The record was set at the Beggin' Pet Parade in St Louis, Missouri, USA.

Meanwhile, the record for **most dogs in a costume parade** was set by Petco Animal Supplies in San Diego, California, USA, in 2011.This Harley hound (right) was just one of 337 dogs to take part in the procession.

Holy whiskers! A dwarf Siamese rabbit named Joey dresses as Batman's sidekick Robin at a Halloween costume parade in Long Beach, California, USA.

Vladimir, a sleek Russian Blue, makes a fine-looking "Bat-cat" for Halloween. Watch out, "Joker-cats" of Gotham City!

It took three attempts to make the perfect "spider-dog" costume.

Olive the pig from Vermont, USA, has some 35,000 followers on Instagram. Here she is dressed as Wonder Woman, looking every inch a super-swine!

In 2014, there were reports of a "mutant giant spider-dog" roaming the streets of Warsaw, Poland... In reality, the scary creature was a sweet dog named Chica in a tarantula costume. The pooch belongs to Polish prankster Sylwester Wardega. The video he filmed of people fleeing in terror when confronted by the eight-legged "monster" was YouTube's biggest hit in 2014. By Mar 2017, Chica's funny vid had received 167.4 million views! Check out more YouTube animal stars on pp.78–79.

DRESSED TO IMPRESS...

Stuck for a costume to wear to your next party? Why not take inspiration from the animal kingdom, as these record-breakers did en masse?

After being counted, the penguins embarked on a 2-km (1.2-mi) waddle around London.

FAST FACT

Ever wondered why penguins have black backs and white bellies? It's actually a form of camouflage. When in the water, their back blends in with the sea from above, while their front blends in with the sky from below.

1 Yateley School in Hampshire, UK, was abuzz with activity on 6 Apr 2011 as 2,176 students flew in from local schools – the **most people dressed as bees**. As well as promoting the importance of these pollinators, the event also raised money to make the campus more bee-friendly.

2 Since the 1940s, the Dallas YMCA Turkey Trot has taken place in Texas, USA, at Thanksgiving. At 2011's event, 661 runners really got into the spirit of the race, setting a record for the **most people dressed as turkeys**. Well, in those outfits, nobody could call them *chicken*!

3 A 624-strong flock huddled in London, UK, on 12 Nov 2015, in celebration of Guinness World Records Day. It was the third year in a row that Richard House Children's Hospice (UK) got their flippers on the title for **most people dressed as penguins**.

4 In honour of their mascot Gorgeous George, the 2 Wish Upon A Star foundation (UK) amassed 385 jumbos at the Principality Stadium in Cardiff, UK, on 13 Aug 2016. It was the **most people dressed as elephants** – and surely a sight *nobody* could forget!

5 The 2009 Denver Gorilla Run was the hairiest to date. A total 1,061 silverback sprinters took on the challenge – the **most people dressed as gorillas**. Organized by the Mountain Gorilla Conservation Fund (USA), the fun run celebrated its 13th year in 2016.

6 A herd of 1,352 people were rustled up at 2014's Deja Moo Country Fair – the **most people dressed as cows**. The festival took place in the aptly named town of *Cow*aramup in Australia. It's also known as "Cowtown" owing to a family of Friesian cattle statues that reside there.

7 Nobody takes animal fancy dress more seriously than "furries". They meet at cosplay events called "con*fur*ences" to celebrate animals in all their forms, with a focus on cartoon critters. A record 2,489 people attended 2006's Anthrocon convention held in Pittsburgh, Pennsylvania, USA – the **largest gathering of furries**.

PEDIGREE CHUMS

When it comes to the world of competitive pet shows, it's dog eat dog – and sometimes cat eat cat! Owners and pets alike are put under the spotlight as judges assess physique, grooming and discipline.

CRUFTS

The **largest dog show** is Crufts, held every year in Birmingham, UK. In 2017 alone, there were 24,263 canine entries from 56 different countries across the four-day event. Dogs go through a rigorous qualification process just to enter, always with their eye on the coveted "Best in Show" cup. The top dog at this year's show was American cocker spaniel Afterglow Miami Ink, pictured below with his owner, Jason Lynn.

The Yorkshire terriers take to their podiums at Crufts 2017.

Based on Best in Show (BiS) wins, the **most successful group at Crufts** is the Gundog group, with 24 wins. The English cocker spaniel (left) is the **most successful Crufts breed**, with seven BiS titles to date: 1930–31, 1938–39, 1948, 1950 and 1996.
At the other end of the scale, the **least successful group at Crufts** is the Toy group, with just three BiS victories. This category includes smaller breeds such as pugs and Chihuahuas (right).

SCRUFFTS

While traditional dog shows are typically reserved for pure-bred pooches, cross-breeds get their chance to shine at "Scruffts". Established in 2000, the UK alternative to Crufts is a little more informal, recognizing categories such as "most handsome dog", "golden oldie" and "child's best friend". In 2013, Scruffts officially became part of Crufts, with the two events running side by side.

Scruffts brings a bit of fun to the serious field of dog events!

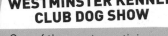
Rumor is only the second herding dog ever to win Best in Show.

WESTMINSTER KENNEL CLUB DOG SHOW

One of the most prestigious events in US pets' diaries is the Westminster Kennel Club Dog Show, which has taken place annually in New York City since 1877. Of the total 2,908 dogs in the 2017 contest, a German shepherd called Rumor (above) walked away with the Best in Show award.

Arguably, the biggest headline at this year's show, however, was the inclusion of cats for the first time. Pedigree felines – such as Jungletrax Abiding Ovation (left) – were exhibited as part of the "Meet the Breeds" side event.

Bengals were just one of 40 cat breeds on display at the 141st Westminster Dog Show in 2017.

SUPREME CAT SHOW

The feline equivalent to the world-famous Crufts event is the Supreme Cat Show. It also takes place in Birmingham, UK, and has been staged by the Governing Council of the Cat Fancy since 1976. Different varieties – including Persians, British and Siamese – face off among their own *cat*-egories before the best of the bunch go head to head. The overall champion is crowned "Best in Show Supreme Exhibit".

FAST FACT
The **oldest dog show** is the UK's Birmingham Dog Show Society Championship Show. Starting in 1859, it's still running as of 2017.

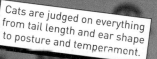
Cats are judged on everything from tail length and ear shape to posture and temperament.

The **most successful breed at the Supreme Cat Show** is the auburn Turkish Van, a semi-longhair, which has won Best in Show three times. On two of these occasions, the top spot was claimed by the very same cat. Akdamar Bazisey Mahsus – owned by Mrs J Johnson (UK) – was placed first two years running: 1995 and 1996.

SHOW GOATS

Goats are gods in Lithuania. Or at least in the village of Ramygala, which adopted the animal as its mascot several centuries ago. Competition at the annual beauty pageant is stiff – there's always a new *kid* on the block!

1

The winner of the 2016 Ramygala goat pageant was a 16-month-old female named Demyte ("Little Spot"). Her owner, Ferdinandas Petkevicius (left), is a retired vet. He entered the contest six years in a row, and this was his first win. After much beautifying with roses on her head, Demyte looked even more fetching in her winner's crown (below). The only thing her owner hadn't had time to do was polish her nails!

Entrants are judged on many criteria, including quality of coat.

FACTS
at your FINGERTIPS

Along with sheep, goats were the first animals to be domesticated by humans, in around 9,000 BCE.

A male goat is called a buck or billy, a female is called a doe or nanny. Young goats are called kids. Babies are up and walking just minutes after being born.

Mountain goats (as opposed to domestic goats) can jump 12 ft (3.6 m) in one leap. The wide spread of their cloven hooves gives them excellent grip.

There were six finalists at 2016's pageant. They were paraded in front of the jury, which comprised the local member of parliament, a headteacher and a cucumber farmer. Prizes included cakes, honey, books and hair-salon coupons.

Seeing the goats' decorations, one onlooker described the pageant as being like a fairytale.

BIZARRE BEAUTY CONTESTS

A goat is made ready for the 2015 pageant. Ramygala was named "goat capital" in the 16th century, and from then adopted the animal as its symbol. This annual event celebrating the horned beasts draws hundreds of people.

It's a matter of beauty and the beasts in Rohtak, India. In a bid to promote local cattle breeds, in 2016 hundreds of cows and bulls were judged for their size and looks, the length of their horns and the cows' milk yield.

I just hope my kids don't see this...

The winner of the 2015 pageant was a goat called Marce. Here, she and her owner, Saverija Dobrovolskiene, do a victory dance in front of the crowd. Saverija later wore the crown when Marce gruffly refused it!

A Serama chicken puffs out its chest in a table-top competition in Kuala Lumpur, Malaysia. This bantam breed, raised for its tiny size and unusual posture, is the **smallest breed of chicken**.

Event organizer Loreta Kubiliuniene inspects a young goat during the 2016 pageant. The celebration also includes a marching band, costumed dancers and a human "king" and "queen" (left) who oversee proceedings.

BEST IN SHOW

The British Tarantula Society run an annual contest known as the "Crufts for spiders". In 2016, Aphrodite (right) was the winner. Among 50,000 entrants, she stood out for her glistening coat and perfect pose.

Pet weddings

You are cordially invited to browse this heartwarming album of animal (rom)antics... If these unconventional brides and grooms can teach us anything, it's that love is in the h-air!

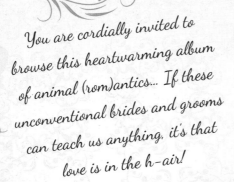

Feline sweethearts Phet and Ploy did nothing by halves when they got hitched in 1996. Phet, the groom, arrived at the ceremony by helicopter, while his bride was dropped off in a Rolls-Royce car! The total cost of the unusual union came to a whopping $39,443 (£25,230), making it the **most expensive pet wedding** to date. The couple were known as "diamond eye" cats, as both shared a rare form of "glaucoma" in which a blueish film forms over the surface of the eyes.

Aunt Bea the pug was just one of 178 brides to wed their *paw*-fect partners at the **largest dog wedding ceremony** on 19 May 2007. The Bow Wow Vows event was organized by the Aspen Grove Lifestyle Center and took place in Littleton, Colorado, USA. It was somewhat of a last-minute marriage, with most of the newlyweds only meeting on the day! Still, there was time to prepare a special pooch-themed cake, complete with icing dogs (see above left).

Following a blind date, bride Huang Pu-pu and groom Shui Fu-ko from Chinese Taipei, tied the knot in 2007. Their owners brought them together to mark the upcoming Year of the Pig. If this weren't bizarre enough, the "best man" and "maid of honour" at the ceremony were parrots!

In 2011, a pair of romantic rabbits wearing traditional Chinese wedding dress got married in Hong Kong. Wonder how many *carrots* were in the bride's ring?!

Three years after his mate died in an accident, there was a happy ending for Pangpang the pelican. Keepers at National Forest Park in Fuzhou, China, introduced him to his new bride Yuanyuan on their wedding day. It was love at first peck!

Mia and Jimmy the hedgehogs add their paw prints to a certificate to make their symbolic wedding official on Valentine's Day in 2015. They were the first of hundreds of animals to declare their love in Lima, Peru. Cats, rabbits and even snakes also walked – or slithered – up the aisle to exchange their vows.

ANIMALS DO THE FUNNIEST THINGS!

Each year, the Comedy Wildlife Photography Awards sets out to show that nature doesn't always have to be serious – it also has a sense of humour! Laugh out loud at our top pick of the finalists from the 2016 competition.

② Heads included, king penguins are the second-largest penguin species.

Hunting voles always gives me brain freeze!

FUR-THER INFO

The Comedy Wildlife Photography Awards was set up in 2014. The big idea was to create a photography contest that didn't take itself too seriously, but there is also a noble cause behind it. Working with the Born Free Foundation, they encourage "conservation through competition", raising the profile of endangered species while also raising a smile.

① Red fox by Angela Bohlke
The overall winner of 2016's Comedy Wildlife Photography Awards was this hilarious picture of a face-planting fox. The snap was captured in the USA's Yellowstone National Park, while the fox hunted for rodents beneath the snow.

② King penguins by Charles Kinsey
Don't panic: these penguins haven't lost their heads – they're just keeping clean. Double-jointed necks let these birds perform this tricky move. The dextrous duo reside on the chilly island of South Georgia in the Atlantic Ocean.

③ Green frog by Artyom Krivosheev
This friendly frog didn't need telling twice to put on a *hoppy* face... The amphibian was spotted in a pond in Lipetsk, Russia. Frogs often gape like this to help them breathe, but to us it looks as if they're smiling.

Eagles and bears don't have much in common but do share a love of fish!

How dare you laugh at me! *En garde!*

④ Plains zebra by Alison Mees
While the photographer was passing a herd of zebra in Ngorongoro Crater, Tanzania, this male pulled a toothy grin. Alison is originally from the UK but moved to Zambia several years ago, following her love for Africa and wildlife.

⑤ Brown bear by Adam Parsons
Bears were a hugely popular subject in 2016, with no fewer than four comedy bears making the shortlist! This snap of a swimming grizzly being photo-bombed by an eagle was Highly Commended by the judges.

⑥ Snowy owl by Edward Kopeschny
Striking a balance between cute and smug is this snowy owl from Ontario, Canada. This species is the **most northerly owl**, found as far north as the Arctic Circle. However, this particular "Hedwig" seems content just chilling out for photos!

⑦ Fan-throated lizard by Anup Deodhar
Warrior of the Grassland was Highly Commended. The male fan-throated lizard from Maharashtra State, India, looks ready to fight off any rivals. The photo was also a finalist in the UK's Wildlife Photographer of the Year competition.

ANIMAL SNAPPERS

There's nothing shy and retiring about these wild posers. They've discovered how fun it is to take pictures (or get someone else to) – and in the process they've mastered the art of the selfie!

I wonder how many likes on Instagram I'll get for this selfie...

FAST FACT

Don't be fooled by the cheeky grin! Celebes crested macaques don't always look as friendly as this... These monkeys will bare their long canines in a grimace if they want to appear threatening.

"Monkey selfie" was one of Google's top 10 most searched terms in 2015!

The selfies taken by this macaque monkey in 2011 went viral. Six-year-old Ella snapped herself in the jungle of Sulawesi, Indonesia, with a camera set up by British photographer David Slater. Who could have guessed that these fun snaps would spark the **first copyright case filed on behalf of an animal**? The People for the Ethical Treatment of Animals (PETA) argued that it was Naruto – another monkey – rather than Ella, or even Slater, who owned the pictures. A judge disagreed, but nevertheless Ella's selfies became famous all round the globe.

WILD PHOTO-BOMBERS

Allan has taken selfies with more than 30 different species to date.

Self-proclaimed "animal whisperer" Allan Dixon from Ireland has made furry friends all over the globe. Posing for the perfect selfie with his beastly buddies takes anywhere between five minutes and three hours. Allan is especially fond of quokkas (top) – tree-climbing marsupials from Australia. Is he the *real* Dr Dolittle?

While diving off Hawaii, USA, Regan Mizuguchi found himself with a pufferfish for a head when the spiky sea creature floated into frame.

Watch the birdie...! A red squirrel photographing a blue tit? Can it be true? Human photographer Vadim Trunov captured magical moments like these in a forest near Voronezh in Russia.

His trick was to sprinkle seeds and nuts around a camera to tempt the woodland creatures to investigate. He would then wait – often for several days – for the perfect shot.

They're nuts for each other! A cheeky ground squirrel got in on the action when newly engaged couple Kelin Flanagan and Spencer Taubner were photographed in Canada's Banff National Park.

It's not only humans that get photo-bombed by animals... As this water buffalo was posing for a serious portrait, little did he know his shot was about to get crashed by a cheeky oxpecker!

THE CUTEST ZOO DOWN UNDER?

Who could resist a cuddle with a koala as adorable as this? At Lone Pine Koala Sanctuary in Queensland, Australia, you don't have to resist – getting up close to these loveable marsupials is all part of the visit! Discover everything you need to know about this record-breaking park and its star residents on pp.166–67.

AT THE ZOO

THE WORLD'S LARGEST ZOO

Opened in 1844 with 850 animals from the king's collection, Zoo Berlin is Germany's oldest animal park. It's also the **largest zoo by species** – home to 19,439 individual animals from 1,354 different species as of 19 Jan 2017.

The iconic 1899 entrance features two life-size elephant statues!

One of Zoo Berlin's most modern pieces of architecture is the Hippo House. Built in 1996, its two glass domes cover exotic plants and a pair of circular pools, where the inhabitants love to wallow. There are even observation windows below the water line, allowing visitors to see how graceful these big beasts can be. Other big mammals at the zoo include elephants, rhinos and giraffes (below).

MAMMAL
1 4 8
SPECIES

These counters reveal the number of species for each animal group at Zoo Berlin.

The Antelope House where the giraffes live was inspired by a mosque's design.

The zoo's reptilian residents live mainly on the first floor of the Aquarium. The terrarium features a wide variety of snakes, turtles and lizards – including the Komodo dragon, the world's **largest lizard**. Crocodile Hall – home to species such as the spectacled caiman (left) – is the centrepiece of the building, visible from all three floors.

REPTILE
0 6 0
SPECIES

Sea lions are famous for their agility and playful nature.

Some of the park's most popular mammals are the California sea lions. Their acrobatic displays are among the highlights of any visit. These animals are as smart as they are nimble; one resident, named Sandra, knows 80 tricks!

FISH
4 9 3
SPECIES

Must find out what blusher she uses...

On the ground floor of the Aquarium, fishy stars include hammerhead sharks, rays and moray eels. This stripy customer is another standout. It's a humphead cichlid from Lake Tanganyika in Africa. They can grow 30 cm (12 in) long and are named after the fatty bump above their eyes.

Some of the most colourful of Zoo Berlin's 1,757 total birds are the flamingos. They get their distinct pink plumage from a substance in their diet called "beta-carotene". The majority of the zoo's avian inhabitants live in the World of Birds exhibit, in which many of them fly free. The zoo also hosts a colony of king penguins in their own dedicated enclosure.

FAST FACT
On the same floor as the amphibians is Zoo Berlin's extensive collection of invertebrates (e.g., insects), made up of 308 species.

When courting, flamingos dance and preen each other.

BIRD
3 0 6
SPECIES

The top storey of the Aquarium is the zoo's amphibian domain. It's home to toads, frogs, newts and salamanders. One of its record-breaking residents is the Australian white-lipped tree frog (right) – the largest tree frog – which can grow to 14 cm (5.5 in) long.

AMPHIBIAN
0 3 9
SPECIES

RECORD-BREAKING ZOOS

Where would you expect to have the wildest time: at a reptilian retreat, a butterfly-filled paradise or a zoo built for an emperor? Whichever you choose, these superlative zoos are all doing their bit for conservation and bringing nature a little closer to home.

REPTILE GARDENS

Slithering serpents, exotic lizards and huge tortoises await visitors at Reptile Gardens, the **largest reptile zoo**. Located in South Dakota, USA, it houses 225 different reptile species – as well as a few other animals – overseen by fearless head keeper Terry Phillip (right).

Reptile Gardens was set up in 1937 by Earl Brockelsby, a 21-year-old snake enthusiast.

The **longest Burmese python** was a female named Baby, who reached a length of 5.74 m (18 ft 10 in). An albino variety of the species hangs out here with staffer Clint.

The **largest toad** is the cane or marine toad, native to South America. An average specimen weighs 450 g (1 lb) – Megan needs both hands to hold this hefty hopper!

A veiled chameleon sits on Virginia's head. The Yemen veiled chameleon is the **smallest veiled chameleon subspecies**, with males as short as 43 cm (16.9 in).

GUINNESS WORLD RECORDS

FAST FACT
The Schönbrunn zoo's first live giraffe, which arrived in 1828 as a gift from Egypt, had a big impact on Viennese society. Dresses, accessories and hairstyles à la giraffe all became popular!

This hand-tinted image shows visitors at Schönbrunn's monkey house, c. 1900.

TIERGARTEN SCHÖNBRUNN

The Tiergarten Schönbrunn in Vienna, Austria, is the **oldest continuously operated zoo**. It was created as a royal menagerie in 1752 by the Holy Roman Emperor Francis I, before opening to the public in 1779. Recently, the zoo's four giraffes were temporarily moved to nearby army barracks while their enclosure got a makeover!

TIERPARK HAGENBECK

The **oldest zoo without bars** is in Hamburg, Germany, and was founded in 1907 by fishmonger's son and animal collector Carl Hagenbeck. He came up with the idea of using deep pits, moats and large pens instead of cages to separate animals from each other and from visitors. For the first time, zoo-goers could see the beasts without barriers!

PENANG BUTTERFLY FARM

Flit over to the Malaysian island of Penang to find the world's **largest butterfly farm**. Opened in 1986 and roughly the size of a soccer pitch, it contains more than 4,000 fluttering residents belonging to 50 different species. On site, there's also a breeding centre and a laboratory.

POLAR PARK

You've got a fair chance of seeing the amazing Northern Lights at the Polar Park Arctic Wildlife Centre in Bardu, Norway. Located at a latitude of 68°69'N, it's the world's **most northerly zoo**. Visitors to this supervised wilderness come face to face with human-friendly, hand-reared wolves (left). You can also track down bears, lynx, moose, elk, reindeer and other cold-climate animals.

AMAZING AQUARIUMS

A record-breaking aquarium has to be a little grander than your average goldfish bowl! Just like the habitats they are imitating, these water worlds are home to a huge range of aquatic creatures – some of which are record holders in their own right.

The **largest aquarium tank** holds the same amount of water as nine Olympic swimming pools! It's part of the huge Hengqin Ocean Kingdom – the world's **largest aquarium** – in Guangdong Province, China. Such a big tank is needed to accommodate the resident whale sharks (see below).

Among the star attractions at Hengqin Ocean Kingdom (above) are the whale sharks – the **largest fish** (below). The biggest to date was found off Pakistan in 1949, measuring 12.65 m (41 ft 6 in) long. The same specimen was also the **heaviest fish**, weighing 21.5 tonnes (47,400 lb) – about the same as three *T. rexes*!

NO WAY!
Whale sharks can be as long as a school bus!

You only eat plankton, right?

Dominating the lobby of the Radisson Blu Hotel in Berlin, Germany, the AquaDom is the **largest cylindrical aquarium**. The tank contains a staggering 1 million litres (264,000 US gallons) of water and around 1,500 fish. Its most unusual feature is an elevator housed in a see-through tube, offering guests a fish-eye view without getting wet.

The elevator car can hold up to 48 passengers at one time.

The centrepiece of Aviapark in Moscow, Russia, is the **tallest cylindrical aquarium**. The three-storey tank at the heart of Europe's biggest shopping mall stands 20.3 m (66 ft 7 in) tall – about the same height as the White House. The hundreds of inhabitants gobble up 8 kg (17 lb 10 oz) of fish food every day.

Horseshoe crabs are some of the oldest creatures on Earth today – with a history spanning at least 445 million years! You can see these ancient animals up close – and even feel them – at the Discovery Centre in Ripley's Aquarium of Canada in Toronto, Ontario. Covering an area of roughly 37.9 m² (407.9 sq ft), the exhibit is the **largest horseshoe crab touch tank**.

FAST FACT
The amazing AquaDom is also the **tallest aquarium with an elevator**. The journey covers a vertical distance of 25 m (82 ft) through the fish-filled tank and lasts for five minutes.

A team of four divers clean the huge fish tank every day!

The touch tank is home to 65 Atlantic horseshoe crabs – the **largest horseshoe crabs**.

LOL PANDA

WHAT GOES BLACK, WHITE, BLACK, WHITE, BLACK, WHITE, BLACK, WHITE?

A PANDA ROLLING DOWN A HILL!

The staff at this panda sanctuary in China don't have a lot of choice when it comes to what they wear at work: the only option is black and white! Joking aside, these unusual uniforms have played an important part in bringing these beautiful bears back from the brink of extinction.

Costumes are a serious business when it comes to panda conservation.

No, it's not fancy-dress day at the zoo... Inside these fuzzy suits are some of the world-leading experts on pandas. So why are they dressed up? It's to help re-introduce cubs into the wild by distancing them from human contact.

QUICK QUIZ

Q. WHAT'S THE NAME FOR A GROUP OF PANDAS?

A. AN EMBARRASSMENT

It's time for a check-up for this cub!

Although taken off the endangered list in 2016, there are still only about 1,900 giant pandas in the wild. Places like the Wolong Panda Center in China are working hard to ensure that the positive trend continues. The centre is part of the Sichuan Giant Panda Sanctuaries – a 9,245-km² (3,569-sq-mi) network of nature reserves that make up the planet's **largest giant panda habitat**.

MONIUM!

To help young pandas adapt to life outside the sanctuary, they can't have any human contact. That's why the keepers here dress up like adult pandas – so that the cubs don't get used to being handled by people. They even go so far as to spray the outfits with panda wee to make them smell like the real thing!

I'm not sure about our new neighbours...

The keepers use CCTV cameras to closely watch the newly released cubs. They also make regular check-ups – dressed in the panda costume, of course! – to monitor the bears' health and well-being.

The cubs start off in a training camp that is semi-wild. Here, it's hoped that the young pandas will learn the skills they need to survive, such as climbing trees and foraging for food. Once they get the hang of things, they're moved to a more remote part of the forest to live with other wild pandas.

NO WAY!
Pandas were not heard of in the West until 1869!

Pandas are transferred between different areas of the reserve in bamboo boxes.

FACTS AT YOUR FINGERTIPS

Giant pandas are the **hungriest bears**, spending up to 16 hr a day munching bamboo. They need to consume about 20 kg (44 lb) daily – roughly the same weight as 83 Big Macs!

Pandas have an extra digit to help tear down bamboo, plus an extra molar tooth to crunch through the tough shoots. They also have thick mucus in their stomachs to protect against splinters.

Cubs are born completely white, only developing their famous black-and-white colouring after a few months.

DATA FILE

COMMON NAME:
Giant panda

SCIENTIFIC NAME:
Ailuropoda melanoleuca
("black-and-white cat foot")

TYPE: Mammal

LOCATION: Central China

WEIGHT: 70–120 kg (154–265 lb)

LOOK WHO'S TALKING...

Humans aren't the only animals with the gift of the gab. Whether communicating by sign language, sounds or symbols, there are some chatty creatures out there with a lot to get off their chests...

GORILLA

Koko is one of the most famous gorillas in the world. Born in San Francisco Zoo, the 46-year-old female is the **most skilled gorilla in sign language**. She can make sense of some 2,000 words of spoken English, and knows over 1,000 signs of "Gorilla Sign Language", having been taught since she was a baby by Dr Francine "Penny" Patterson (left). When Koko was asked if she was an animal or a person, the clever ape replied: "Fine animal gorilla."

As you can see, the pair are very close after more than 40 years together. Koko herself is an animal lover, too – she is a huge fan of kittens!

Koko "adopted" her first kitten in the 1980s – she named it All Ball.

SPOTTED DOLPHIN

After 25 years working with Atlantic spotted dolphins, Denise Herzing and her team made a breakthrough. The researchers had used a computer to create a series of whistles, hoping that the marine mammals might start using them as part of their vocabulary. While swimming with the pod in 2013, Denise recorded one of the dolphins making the whistle for "seaweed".

Did someone order seaweed?

FAST FACT
Penny used several techniques to teach Koko sign language. This included "modelling" (demonstrating a sign for Koko to copy) and "molding" (positioning Koko's hands into the correct shape).

HORSE

And now for the *mane* event! In 2010, rescue horse Lukas achieved the **most numbers identified by a horse in one minute**: 19. His owner, Karen Murdock, taught him numbers using a combination of repetition and rewards. Lukas is no one-trick pony – he can also pick out letters and recognize colours.

GUINNESS
WORLD RECORDS

CERTIFICATE

The most numbers correctly identified
by a horse in one minute is 19
and was achieved by 'Lukas',
who was assisted by his owner and trainer
Karen Murdock (USA)
at Walnut, CA, USA,
on 16 June 2010

GUINNESS WORLD RECORDS LTD

Merlin from Torquay, UK, boasts the **loudest purr by a domestic cat**. His purr has been clocked at 67.8 decibels – about the same volume as a vacuum cleaner!

67.8 dB

The **loudest species of parrot** is the salmon-crested cockatoo from Indonesia. Their shrieks have been recorded reaching 135 decibels!

135 dB

BUDGIE

Budgerigars are among the most talkative of all birds. The **bird with the largest vocabulary ever** was a budgie called Puck, owned by Camille Jordan of Petaluma, California, USA. Before he passed away in 1994, Puck knew an incredible 1,728 words!

BONOBO

Kanzi the bonobo communicates with Dr Sue Savage-Rumbaugh via pages filled with symbols. The male ape knows the meaning of 3,000 spoken English words and can also perform "human" activities, such as lighting fires to cook food.

The **loudest bark by a dog** measured 113.1 decibels – louder than a revving motorcycle! It was produced by a golden retriever named Charlie in Adelaide, Australia. Talk about *hound* effects...

113.1 dB

Kanzi picked up some sign language after watching videos of Koko (left)!

NEW ARRIVALS

If you're a sucker for baby animals, you need to add ZooBorns to your favourites list! The blog, set up by lifelong "animal nerd" Andrew Bleiman and visual artist Chris Eastland, celebrates the latest – and most adorable – zoo residents.

① *Bambi's got nothing on me!*

Chester Zoo, UK

② Taronga Zoo, Australia

In a meerkat mob, the whole family gets involved with rearing the young.

③ La Palmyre Zoo, France; photo by Florence Perroux

FUR-THER INFO

For nearly a decade, ZooBorns has showcased the newest, cutest baby animals born at accredited zoos and aquariums. But these babies aren't just adorable faces... They also serve as ambassadors for their wild cousins, educating the public on the conservation challenges faced by their species. In addition to the popular online media outlet, ZooBorns has published a number of books. Find out more at **www.zooborns.com**.

ZooBorns

① Dik-dik
In Feb 2017, this adorable, doe-eyed dik-dik was being bottle-fed by zoo staff. The tiny antelope's mother had died soon after the birth. African bush-dwelling dik-diks are so-called after the sound of the alarm calls made by females.

② Meerkats
Who could resist those eyes? Six pups made up the largest meerkat litter this Sydney-based zoo has ever had: previous litters were just two-strong. Native to the plains of southern Africa, meerkats have nothing to do with cats, but belong to the mongoose family.

③ Golden lion tamarins
La Palmyre Zoo on the west coast of France welcomed two golden lion tamarins – named after their manes – in 2016. While these tiny monkeys are still endangered in their native Brazil, recent conservation efforts are seeing numbers rise.

GUINNESS WORLD RECORDS

④

Royal Burgers' Zoo, Netherlands;
photo by Theo Kruse

A fennec fox's huge ears radiate body heat, helping to keep it cool in its native desert home.

⑤

Taronga Zoo, Australia

FAST FACT
Young cheetah cubs have a grey "mantle" of fur. To human eyes this halo of fluff makes them look even more cuddly, but it likely serves as camouflage in the wild. The mantle is shed as the cubs grow older.

⑥

Antwerp Zoo, Belgium; photo by Jonas Verhulst

LOL
WHAT DO YOU CALL A BABY BEAR WITH NO TEETH?

A GUMMY BEAR!

⑦

Chester Zoo, UK

④ **Cheetahs**
The cheetah is the **fastest mammal on land**, but this busy mum wasn't going anywhere: she had six cubs to look after! Cheetah numbers in the wild are in decline, so this large litter born at Royal Burgers' Zoo in 2017 was a huge breakthrough.

⑤ **Fennec fox**
Fennec fox babies are so cute that ZooBorns – experts in cuteness – have one in their logo! A cub was recently born at Taronga Zoo, where at two months old it was just beginning to sample crickets and mice... Fennecs are the world's **smallest foxes**.

⑥ **Blue-spotted stingray**
In early 2017, this Belgian animal park welcomed a male blue-spotted stingray "pup". It will soon be feeding on eels, like the adults. Native to Asia, these rays have venomous tail barbs, so predators – and divers – are best to give them a wide berth!

⑦ **Malayan tapir**
A relation of the rhino, this is the **largest tapir species**, growing to between 6 and 8 ft (1.8–2.4 m) long. But newborn Solo was still a slip of a thing pictured here in 2016. After about a year he will lose his stripy pattern and his coat will become half black and half white.

HOW OLD?!

Protected from the hazards of the wild – predators, food shortages, harsh weather – most creatures are likely to live longer in zoos. But these long-lived beasts have exceeded all expectations! Meet some of the animal kingdom's most senior citizens of all time...

3 m (10 ft 10 in)

FAST FACT

Manatees are herbivores and can eat a tenth of their own weight in 24 hr! Snooty snacks on 70–80 lb (32–36 kg) of fruit and veg per day. It's a crunchy diet of lettuce, carrots, kale, cabbage, broccoli, sweet potato and apples.

SNOOTY

Born in 1948, Snooty is the **oldest manatee in captivity**. Aged 68 as of Mar 2017, he came to the South Florida Museum when he was an 11-month-old calf. In the wild, most manatees live for 30–40 years, though one is known to have reached 59. A number of rescued "sea cows" have come to share Snooty's pool before being put back into the ocean. As he was hand-reared from birth, Snooty wouldn't survive if released into the wild. Instead, he's formed close ties with his human handlers and has also amassed an online following thanks to his own personal webcam!

DATA FILE

COMMON NAME:
West Indian manatee

SCIENTIFIC NAME:
Trichechus manatus

TYPE: Mammal

LOCATION: Florida, USA; Greater Antilles; northern South America

WEIGHT: Up to 590 kg (1,300 lb)

DIVING DURATION:
Up to 20 min on a single breath

Record-setting Snooty is also the official mascot of Manatee County in Florida!

IVORY

Ivory has made film and TV appearances with the likes of Angelina Jolie, Usher and 50 Cent.

Often called a black panther, Ivory is, in fact, an African leopard with "melanism" – an abnormal amount of dark pigment in the skin and fur. Aged 25 in Mar 2017, he's the **oldest leopard in captivity**. Reared as a performer, he's one of the veteran stars of Steve Martin's Working Wildlife animal acting school in California, USA.

LITTLE MAMA

Based on an age assessment by acclaimed primate expert Jane Goodall, Little Mama is thought to be 77 years old as of Mar 2017. That makes her the **oldest chimpanzee in captivity**. The elderly great ape has lived at Lion Country Safari in Florida, USA, since 1967, when the park opened. She had previously been a performer with travelling variety show the "Ice Capades".

PATRICK

Orphaned as a baby, Patrick the bare-nosed wombat was only around eight months old when he arrived at the Ballarat Wildlife Park in Victoria, Australia. He went on to lead a long and happy life there for more than three decades, until he sadly passed away in Apr 2017. Estimated to be as old as 31, this easily makes Pat the **oldest wombat in captivity ever**. The average life span of these burrowing marsupials is just 10–15 years in the wild and around 20 years in zoos.

Patrick the wombat has more than 57,000 likes on his Facebook page!

I can't wait till I'm grown up...

I wish I was younger...

COLO

In 1956, Colo became the **first gorilla born in captivity**. Columbus Zoo in Powell, Ohio, USA, was her birthplace, and home for the rest of her life ("Colo" is short for "Columbus, Ohio"). The western lowland gorilla died peacefully in early 2017 – departing with another record, as the **oldest gorilla in captivity ever**.

A great-great-grandmother, she celebrated her 60th birthday a month before her death, outliving the average gorilla by at least 20 years! Her party picnic (right) included a cake made out of apples and tomatoes – two of her favourite fruits.

Colo was mother of three, grandmother of 16, great-grandmother of 12 and great-great-grandmother of three!

CRAZY ABOUT KOALAS!

Australia's Lone Pine Koala Sanctuary was founded in 1927. This easily makes it the planet's **oldest koala sanctuary**. As well as 130 or so koalas, the Queensland-based park is also home to a wide range of other Australian wildlife.

LONE PINE
KOALA SANCTUARY
The World's First & Largest Koala Sanctuary

When Europeans first saw koalas, they thought they had found a new species of bear. It's easy to see why! Although sometimes still called "koala bears", they're actually relatives of kangaroos and wombats. It's time to get to know one of Australia's cutest critters...

A curved backbone and small ribcage let koalas really curl up!

Powerful thigh muscles help with climbing.

NO WAY!

A newborn koala is about the size of a grape!

Two thumb-like digits and long claws are great for gripping.

A tough hide and thick fur make sitting in trees more comfortable.

The koala is very particular when it comes to food. In fact, it's widely considered the animal kingdom's **fussiest eater**. Not only does it exclusively eat the foliage of just one type of tree – eucalyptus – but the leaves have to be of a particular age. Eucalyptus is toxic to most animals, but these marsupials have evolved specialized digestive systems to overcome this.

Koalas are rarely seen drinking as they get all the water they need from the leaves they eat.

One of the biggest draws to Lone Pine is the chance to snuggle one of the star residents! To make sure that the koalas don't get stressed out, the staff keep close tabs on hug time so that no individual koala is handled for more than 30 min per day.

Just another five hours and I'll get up...

Few animals enjoy a good nap more than koalas. In fact, they are the **sleepiest marsupial**, spending as long as 18 hr in the land of nod per day! They tend to wedge themselves into the junction between a branch and the trunk of a tree to avoid falling out.

FAST FACT

Koalas are well-adapted to life in the treetops, so rarely venture to the ground, where they are slow and vulnerable. That said, they are surprisingly strong swimmers, which comes in handy if caught in a flood.

DATA FILE

COMMON NAME: Koala

SCIENTIFIC NAME: *Phascolarctos cinereus*

TYPE: Marsupial (group of mammals whose babies finish developing outside the mother's body – often in a pouch)

LOCATION: Australia

WEIGHT: Up to 13 kg (28 lb 10 oz)

LENGTH: Up to 90 cm (35 in)

In general, koalas live for about 16 years in captivity. But a female born at the Lone Pine park in 1978 defied the odds. Sarah (right) was 23 years old when she died in 2001, which easily makes her the **oldest koala ever**.

DOUBLE TROUBLE

Like the young of all marsupials, baby koalas are called joeys. For the most part, females have no more than one joey each year. However, there have been rare instances of twins, which is the **largest koala litter**. The first recorded identical koala twins were Euca and Lyptus, born in Queensland, Australia, in 1999. The cute duo pictured here are Kialla and Tahilla from Wildlife Wonderland park in Victoria, Australia, who were born in 2009.

LONDON ZOO STOCKTAKE

Once a year, keepers at ZSL London Zoo in the UK dust off their calculators and clipboards to count up the residents. In 2017, Guinness World Records was invited along to the census...

For obvious reasons, ZSL staff keep *very* close tabs on animal numbers throughout the year. However, the annual stocktake is the perfect chance to officially log their list of inhabitants with the international body that approves the zoo's licence each year.

Here, Suzi Hyde is tallying the flippered residents on Penguin Beach. London Zoo's penguin pool is the largest of its kind in England. With the arrival of four new chicks in 2016, the latest penguin populace stands at 78: all of these are Humboldt penguins, except for one rockhopper called Ricky (inset).

HUMBOLDT
0 7 7
PENGUINS

You can count on me!

ROCKHOPPER
0 0 1
PENGUIN

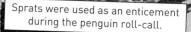

Sprats were used as an enticement during the penguin roll-call.

Some animals move so fast that it can be hard to keep track of who has been logged! To help, the zoo sometimes introduces a distraction to encourage them to stay still. Often this is in the form of food, but in the case of the naturally curious meerkats, they brought in an outsized abacus! The counting tool also came in handy for keeper Veronica Heldt, who could use it to double-check that all of the meerkats were present and correct!

QUICK QUIZ

Q. WHAT DO YOU CALL A GROUP OF MEERKATS?

A. A MOB

0 0 4
MEERKATS

Some keepers get the short straw during the stocktake... Sam Aberdeen (right) from the BUGS exhibit was tasked with counting all the *Partula* snails. Not only do these number in the thousands, but the juveniles can be as tiny as 1–2 mm (0.04–0.08 in) long! The snails are kept in their own special room where the temperature and humidity can be controlled. Anyone entering the *Partula* pad also has to put on a lab coat to keep out any contaminants.

100%

PARTULA
2 1 3 2
SNAILS

ZSL London is part of a worldwide conservation effort to breed *Partula* snails and return them to the wild.

ZSL LONDON ZOO
ANNUAL STOCKTAKE
2017
JAE JAE ✓
MELATI ✓
ACHILLES ✓
KARIS ✓

The tigers love perfume, so it's often sprayed around their enclosure to help keep them entertained!

SUMATRAN
0 0 4
TIGERS

In 2016, ZSL London Zoo's population of Sumatran tigers doubled. Adult female Melati has lived in Tiger Territory since 2011, joined by male Jae Jae a year later. The pair had three cubs in 2014, all of which have now moved to other zoos as part of an international breeding initiative for this critically endangered feline. Last year, Melati gave birth to two new cubs – Achilles (left) and Karis, who love getting up to mischief!

An annual stocktake has taken place at London Zoo since it opened in 1826. In this photo from 1953, a predecessor to Suzi (see above left) counts heads inside the penguin enclosure. At this time, king penguins were the resident species.

BACTRIAN
0 0 2
CAMELS

FUR-THER INFO

Founded in 1826, ZSL (Zoological Society of London) is an international scientific, conservation and educational charity whose mission is to promote and achieve the worldwide conservation of animals and their habitats. This mission is realized through ground-breaking science, active conservation projects in more than 50 countries and two zoos. To find out more, visit **www.zsl.org**.

Mick Tiley definitely had one of the easier counts of the day... He's in charge of the zoo's Bactrian camel paddock, which has just two tenants: Genghis and Noemi. In the wild, these two-humped beasts are perfectly adapted to life in Asia's Gobi Desert, able to survive for days without food or water and travel for miles.

ZSL | **LET'S WORK FOR WILDLIFE**

ORIGAMI ZOO

Originating in Japan, origami is the art of folding paper into fantastic forms and figures. It works brilliantly with beasts of all varieties – as these record-worthy crafty creations prove.

100%

Some of the origami elephants sent in were as small as a fingernail!

Anyone who contributed to the **largest display of origami elephants** deserves the right to blow their own trumpet! In 2016, the Wildlife Conservation Society gathered 78,564 paper jumbos at the Bronx Zoo in New York, USA. The project aimed to raise awareness about the large number of elephants still being killed by poachers for their ivory. People sent in paper creations from countries all over the globe, including Iran, Kazakhstan and Egypt.

Adjudicator Hannah Ortman counting the thousands of elephants displayed.

The paper crane, or *orizuru*, is the classic origami design. It represents the rare red-crowned crane, which is an important animal in Japanese culture, said to live for 1,000 years! In Nov 2010, Yoneyama Yuichi (right) achieved the record for **fastest time to make 100 paper cranes**. He folded the colourful birds in 40 min 35 sec at the Nishi Yogo public school in Nagoya, Japan. That's an average of just 24.35 sec per crane!

Bats look a lot less spooky when they come in rainbow colours! In 2015, Conner Prairie Interactive History Park put together the **largest display of origami bats**. Made by visitors and staff, a total of 6,239 paper critters fluttered into the museum in Fishers, Indiana, USA.

The froggy display was laid out in a mosaic that depicted more frogs!

Among other things, the Japanese crane is a symbol of peace. In 1999, leaders of the World Peace Project for Children organized the creation of the then **largest origami paper crane**. Made at the Kingdome stadium in Seattle, Washington, USA, by some 800 people, the bird was formed of heavy-duty paper – bearing messages from 10,000 children. The final sculpture stood 120 ft (36.5 m) tall and spanned 215 ft 8 in (65.7 m).

NO WAY!
The crane's wings were as wide as a 747 jumbo jet!

The record for the **largest display of origami frogs** is 1,578. The colourful army of paper amphibians was made by children, parents and staff at the Children's Culture Centre in Kumamoto, Japan. The best thing about origami frogs is that they can be made to jump... which is *croakily* awesome!

TURN OVER TO MAKE YOUR OWN ORIGAMI FROG!

ORIGAMI ZOO

Inspired by our round-up of origami animals on pp.170–71? Then try making one yourself! A sheet of A4 origami paper works best, but you can also use normal printer paper. Just follow the folds to find the frog…

1 Fold the top-left corner to the right, about two-thirds of the way down the right side, then unfold.

2 Fold the top-right corner to the left, then unfold. The creases should now form an "X".

3 Fold the top half of the "X" to the back.

4 Unfold to reveal a pop-up crease running through the centre of the "X".

5 Poke down the centre of the "X" with your finger. The whole piece will collapse into a triangle as it appears in step 5. This will be your frog's head.

FUR-THER INFO

This tutorial was provided by our friends at Origami Way, a papercraft website with easy-to-follow instructions. Now you've made a frog, how about trying your hand at a butterfly, a cat or a panda? Pick your favourite animal and make it come to life! Visit **www.origamiway.com**.

Origami Panda
Difficulty: Medium

Origami Bunny
Difficulty: Medium

Origami Butterfly
Difficulty: Easy-Medium

Flapping Butterfly
Difficulty: Easy

Easy Origami Cat
Difficulty: Easy

Origami Cat
Difficulty: Medium

Easy Origami Dog
Difficulty: Easy

Origami Dog

Origami Way

6 Fold the left and right corners of the triangle to the top to form a "diamond".

7 Next, fold the left and right edges of the paper to the centre.

8 Fold the bottom edge up to the centre of the "diamond".

9 Fold that same edge back on itself to the bottom. Finally, turn the paper over to see the frog shape!

FAST FACT
"Origami" comes from the Japanese words *ori*, meaning "folding", and *kami*, meaning "paper". Traditional Japanese origami has been practised since the Edo period (1603–1868).

Kiss me and maybe I'll turn into a prince!

10 Now it's time to get creative... Decorate your frog with eyes, spots – anything you fancy – and you're finished! The best thing about this paper Kermit is that it even moves like a frog – just press down on its back to make it hop!

MIGHTY MOLLUSC!

Imagine finding one of these in your garden nibbling on your herbs! The African giant land snail truly lives up to its name and its record of **largest terrestrial snail**. The biggest specimen to date was called Gee Geronimo, owned by Christopher Hudson from Hove, UK. At 900 g (2 lb), he was as heavy as a pineapple! When fully stretched out, the gigantic gastropod had a nose-to-tail length of 39.3 cm (15.5 in) – making him quite a handful! You'll meet many more unusual pets in the next chapter...

100%

PECULIAR PETS

BIG PICTURE

TAIL OF THE UNEXPECTED

Cygnus the Maine Coon from Michigan, USA, has a tail even longer than his body! As verified on 28 Aug 2016, his tail measures in at 44.6 cm (17.5 in) – the **longest tail on a domestic cat**. Maine Coons are one of the largest domestic cat breeds in the world, with both the **longest cat (current)** and the **longest cat (ever)** also belonging to the same breed.

Maine Coons are the official "state pet" of Maine, USA.

QUICK QUIZ

Q. WHICH BIG CAT HAS THE LONGEST TAIL IN RELATION TO ITS BODY?

A. SNOW LEOPARD

LOL

WHAT DOES A CAT SAY IF SOMEONE STEPS ON ITS TAIL?

ME-OW!

Check out yet more amazing animals in *Guinness World Records 2018*. It's also packed with lots of human marvels and a special superhero-themed chapter!

GUINNESS WORLD RECORDS 2018

THE BARE BONES

On average, cats have 20–23 vertebrae (back bones) in their tails, decreasing ever smaller from the base to the tip. The tail accounts for almost 10% of a cat's entire skeleton! The high number of bones allow for a greater degree of flexibility. When it comes to record-breaking tails, the measurement is made from the pelvis to the tip of the final bone – excluding the cartilage and fur that extend beyond

TOP 10
BIZARRE BUDDIES

There are certain animals you would never think to put together... right? But there are exceptions. Sometimes friendship wins out, as proven by our pick of the most unlikely BFFs (best friends *fur*-ever).

1 TORTOISE & HIPPO

Mzee the tortoise and Owen the hippopotamus met after the young hippo was traumatically washed out to sea during the 2004 tsunami in the Indian Ocean. Thankfully, he was rescued from a reef and taken to Haller Park wildlife sanctuary in Mombasa, Kenya.

Here, he formed a bond with 130-year-old Mzee, the resident Aldabra tortoise. As well as eating together and snuggling up to sleep, they loved nothing better than to share a mud bath! Now Owen is fully grown, the pair have been separated for safety, but they will remain bizarre buddies for life.

2 CAT & MOUSE

If Tom and Jerry have taught us one thing, it's that cats and mice do *not* mix! But Auan and Jeena from Thailand seem to have ironed out their differences. The peculiar pair have been working wonders for cat-mouse relations; as well as playing and eating together, Auan protects his small companion from larger animals such as dogs.

3 DOLPHIN & DOG

After losing her mate in 2007, Duggie the dolphin found a four-legged friend in Ben the Labrador, who lived in a seaside hotel on Tory Island, off the coast of Ireland. On spotting his flippered fan, Ben would leap off the pier into the sea, where the two would splash and play for hours.

4 BABOON & BUSHBABY

Keepers at Nairobi Animal Orphanage in Kenya were very surprised to see two residents become the best of friends. On arriving at the sanctuary in 2011, a young bushbaby called Gakii was quickly adopted by a female yellow baboon – as if he were her own infant. The primate pals spent virtually all their time together, even sharing meals.

6 MONKEY & CAT

Fate brought together Piek the macaque and Pom the cat, who met at a temple near Bangkok in Thailand. The unlikely duo spent most of their time hanging out, with Piek often grooming Pom's fur for bugs. Monkeys are considered sacred in Thailand, so temples offer a refuge where they are left in peace and are often given free food by the monks.

LOL

WHAT IS A HORSE'S FAVOURITE US STATE?

NEIGH-BRASKA!

5 TIGER & DOG

Proving that dogs *can* get along with cats – even really big ones – are Suria the Siberian tiger and Jenny the German shepherd (below). The pair are very close, having grown up together at a sanctuary in Slovakia. In 2015, their friendship passed down to the next generation when their kids met (above).

7 HORSE & CAT

You won't catch Dakota the horse with a long face when his pal Sappy is nearby. The pair have had a "bromance" ever since Sappy was a kitten. Their owner – Denice Kinney from Illinois, USA – says that Sappy lies on the horse's back and sometimes even runs behind when she and Dakota go out riding.

9 DEER & DOG

In 2015, a real-life Bambi who was found abandoned in a field in Germany at just one week old was rescued by farmers. Knowing that he wouldn't survive on his own, a local family adopted the deer and named him Hansi. The fortunate fawn was an immediate hit with the family's 12-week-old Australian shepherd puppy, Lia; the two have since become the *deer*-est of friends.

8 BEAR, LION & TIGER

Baloo the black bear, Leo the lion and Shere Khan the Bengal tiger were all found in a basement as cubs and moved to Noah's Ark sanctuary in Georgia, USA. The inseparable trio were affectionately known as the "BLT" by the staff. Although Leo sadly passed away in 2016, the other two remain very close.

10 FOX & HOUND

Dogs and foxes are famous enemies, but Juniper and Moose clearly weren't told about past hostilities. Their adorable friendship has played out on social media, where Juniper is the **most followed fox on Instagram**. Juniper's adoptive owners are convinced that she now sees herself as more of a dog than a fox!

PAMPERED POOCHES

We all love our bow-wows, but some owners take doggy-doting to a whole new level. These lucky pets are not known to object, though! If the grooming and shopping sessions all get too much, there's always a velvet couch to chill out on...

LOLA

£600

£120

£75

£450

£1,000

£750

Lola won her "most pampered" crown on UK TV in 2013.

We don't have a record for "most pampered pet", but if we did, one contender would have to be Yorkshire terrier Lola. Owner Louise Harris (inset left) from Chelmsford, UK, has splashed out hundreds of thousands of pounds on grooming, designer clothes and fancy food. Lola's siblings (above) enjoy the same luxury lifestyle and have daytime nannies while their owner works. Above are just a few of the accessories and outfits owned by the high-end hounds – plus their price tags!

Hmm, now to find a muddy puddle...

Golden Rescue in Ontario, Canada, held the **largest dog-grooming lesson** in Sep 2014, with 364 people brushing their hounds. The charity, which finds good homes for unwanted golden retrievers, was set up in 1990 when Penny and Rob Manning took on a "dirty, wild pup", who before long became a perfectly groomed and much-loved pet.

BORA BORA BEACH

At Paradise Ranch Pet Resort in California, USA, dogs roam freely all day, splash in their own water park and sleep on sofas in air-conditioned rooms. If, like Titan (right), your birthday falls during your stay, you'll even get your very own party! One owner summed it up when she said, "My dog is staying in a nicer resort than I am on my vacation!"

A staggering $3.2 m (£2.5 m) is the price tag on this diamond dog collar from La Collection de Bijoux. Its 1,600 gems in a chandelier design will certainly bring a sparkle to those lovely brown eyes.

Goggles for dogs, aka doggles, are the eyewear of choice for cool canines. Not just a fashion accessory, they help to protect eyes from UV light and are very useful when skydiving (see p.65).

TOBY

The **wealthiest dog** was a standard poodle like this one. Toby received a legacy of $15 m (£10.5 m) from his owner, Ella Wendel, in 1931. He continued to live in Ms Wendel's fine New York mansion, looked after by three servants. That was one posh poodle!

In 2013, Rocky the Chihuahua – then Britain's best-dressed dog – became the owner of this bespoke £1,600 ($2,000) bed. An entire range of "Rocky" furniture followed, selling to high-end pets at high-end prices.

LOL
WHERE DO ROYAL DOGS LIVE?
BARKINGHAM PALACE!

BUT ARE THEY HOUSE-TRAINED?!

For most of us, the wildest thing that we'll ever share a house with is a cat or a dog – or perhaps just a goldfish! But now and then, some rather unorthodox "pets" make a place in their owners' homes, as well as their hearts...

I really think pig furniture could take off...

Esther the pig also has a huge Instagram following, with some 346,000 fans. See more Instagr-animals on pp.82–83.

ESTHER

Esther the Wonder Pig just kept growing and growing... No one was more surprised than her owner Steve Jenkins, who thought he'd bought a miniature pig that would be no bigger than a cat! Now she's a mighty 650 lb (295 kg) and they've moved to their own sanctuary in Ontario, Canada.

Esther still prefers life indoors, though – she's a real "people pig", super-intelligent and affectionate. And if you thought that pigs are dirty, think again. Esther can let herself out if she needs the toilet and she likes nothing more than a bath.

STAR, ROANIE & HANIA

Why live in a paddock when you can move in with your owners? Miniature horses Star, Roanie and Hania, who live with Corinna Northover (right) in Derby, UK, have their hooves firmly under the table. The petite ponies stand just 31–34 in (78.7–86.3 cm) tall, so they don't take up much room. After competing in equestrian shows, they certainly deserve some downtime, chilling out in the kitchen with a ready supply of carrots!

Who's been eating my porridge?

Grizzlies need to eat 35 lb (15.8 kg) of food per day.

BRUTUS

Can a huge grizzly be as cuddly as a teddy bear? US naturalist Casey Anderson certainly thinks so. To prove it, Casey adopted Brutus in 2002 as an orphaned cub, and the pair have been inseparable ever since. He was even Casey's best man at his wedding!

The baby bear inspired Casey to found the Montana Grizzly Encounter sanctuary for rescue bears, where Brutus spends most of his time. But sometimes Brutus joins the family indoors for special occasions. Can someone pass the honey?

SI BELANG

The world's **longest species of snake** wouldn't be everyone's first choice of pet, but the Toe family from Borneo were happy to share their home with Si Belang. The 6-m-long (19-ft 8-in) reticulated python was raised by the Toes from a young age, so considered them his family. Si Belang got involved with everything from meals to bathtime (right).

LOL

WHEN HER CALF WENT OFF TO COLLEGE, WHAT DID MUMMY BUFFALO SAY?

BI-SON!

WILD THING

Sherron and RC Bridges share their Texas ranch house with 2,500 lb (1,134 kg) of buffalo. Wild Thing could have wrecked the place, but somehow squeezed in quite neatly, and even has his own room where he likes watching TV (right). RC says it's like having a small car around – only hairier, perhaps?

Wild Thing was the "best man" at RC and Sherron's wedding!

BIG PICTURE

EIGHT-LEGGED GIANT

At 175 g (6.1 oz), Rosi is the world's **heaviest spider**. The female goliath birdeater lives with Walter Baumgartner of Andorf, Austria. Goliath birdeaters are the **largest spider species** in terms of body length and mass, and in the wild can be found in the rainforests of South America. Despite their scary reputation, these tarantulas will only attack a human if threatened, and their venomous bite is not much worse than a wasp's sting. Still, people keeping these colossal creepy-crawlies as pets know that they need to be handled with care...

Menu

Hummingbird hotpot

Toad in the hole

Ratatouille

Serpent soup

Lizard linguine

Beetle balti

FOOD FOR THOUGHT

The goliath birdeater got its name after a Victorian explorer witnessed one eating a hummingbird. In fact, this arachnid rarely eats birds, feeding mainly on ground-dwellers such as earthworms and frogs. But it won't turn its nose up at small rodents, crickets, lizards or even the occasional venomous snake!

QUICK QUIZ

Q. WHAT DO RABBITS AND TARANTULAS HAVE IN COMMON?

A. THEY BOTH LIVE IN BURROWS

PETITE PETS

Watch where you step! These miniature companions have all earned records for their diminutive dimensions. But what they lack in size, they make up for in "aww" factor! To give an idea of just how small they are, we've placed them next to an average-height man.

FAST FACT
All our animal height records are from the ground to the "withers" – the ridge between the shoulders. Unlike the head, this is the highest point of the body that does not move relative to the ground, so it's easier to standardize.

100%

The **shortest dog** in the world is Miracle Milly, a Chihuahua from Dorado in Puerto Rico. Having barely grown any bigger than when she was a pup, Milly measures just 9.6 cm (3.8 in) tall.

Meet Lilieput, the munchkin cat. At a mere 13.3 cm (5.2 in) tall from floor to shoulder, she is currently the **shortest domestic cat**. The former stray was adopted by pet-sitter Christel Young and now lives in Napa, California, USA.

As a rule, Roborovski hamsters from Mongolia grow no longer than 5 cm (1.9 in), making them the **smallest breed of domestic hamster**. They weigh about the same as a single AA battery!

GUINNESS WORLD RECORDS

NO WAY!
KneeHi has fathered regular-size donkeys!

Standing just 44.5 cm (1 ft 5.5 in), Thumbelina is the **shortest horse**. The sorrel brown mare shares Goose Creek Farms in St Louis, Missouri, USA, with several other miniature horses – but none as small as her!

KneeHi is so named because he only reaches 64.2 cm (2 ft 1.2 in) to the withers – that's about knee level for an adult human. The **shortest donkey** resides at Best Friends Farm in Gainesville, Florida, USA, with the Lee family.

TURN OVER FOR PRODIGIOUS PETS!

PRODIGIOUS PETS

You met some of the world's most petite pets on pp.186–87. Now marvel at these record-holding gentle giants! All of them (except the hamster) were measured from the ground to the "withers" – the ridge between the shoulders.

FAST FACT
Arcturus is a Savannah, a cross between a domestic cat and a serval, which is a large-eared wild African cat. The breed has some dog-like characteristics, such as playing in water and learning to fetch.

Zeus the Great Dane, who died in 2014, retains the record for the **tallest dog ever**. He measured 111.8 cm (3 ft 8 in) from ground to withers. When up on his hind legs, he towered over his owner, Denise Doorlag from Otsego, Michigan, USA.

The **tallest domestic cat** is Arcturus Aldebaran Powers from Michigan, USA. At 48.4 cm (1 ft 7 in) as of 3 Nov 2016, he is taller than the previous record holder, Savannah Islands Trouble, by just a whisker.

You'd have to reinvent the hamster wheel to fit this super-sized rodent! At 40 cm (1 ft 3.7 in) in length from head to tail, the black-bellied hamster, as it's also known, is the world's **largest species of hamster**.

Measuring an *ass*tounding 172.7 cm (5 ft 8 in), an American Mammoth Jackstock named Romulus is the **tallest donkey**. He and his brother, Remus, live on a farm in Texas, USA, where they guard the other livestock from predatory coyotes.

As a Belgian draft horse, Big Jake was always going to be, well, big. But standing at 210.1 cm (6 ft 10 in), he is currently the **tallest horse**. That gives him the edge when he competes at equestrian shows in Wisconsin, USA.

WORLD'S TALLEST DOGS

One of the most hotly contested records was recently taken by Freddy the Great Dane from Leigh-on-Sea, UK. At 103.5 cm (3 ft 4.75 in), he is now officially the world's tallest dog. Bow-WOW!

It took our Editor-in-Chief Craig Glenday (below left) and vet Emma Norris (left) the best part of a day to measure Freddy. He may dwarf most adults when on his hind legs, but this four-year-old gentle giant was shy of the measuring stick! He came round to the idea with lots of encouragement from his owner, Claire Stoneman (below right), and a few of his favourite liver-flavoured treats.

Since gaining the title of **tallest dog**, Freddy has had his first taste of the high life: you may have seen him in *Biggest Dog in the World* – a show that aired on British TV in Dec 2016.

NO WAY!

Freddy was the runt of a litter of 13!

As a pup, Freddy devoured 23 sofas! He's now more partial to a whole roast chicken.

HOW TO MEASURE *YOUR* DOG

Think your pooch shows vertical promise? Here's how to do the official legwork yourself, whether the dog in question is an abnormally lofty lurcher or a surprisingly towering terrier...

1 For this record, your dog must be at least one year old and have a clean bill of health.

2 Measuring must be carried out by a qualified vet, with two independent witnesses.

3 Using a professional measuring stick, measure from the base of the front foot to the top of the withers (the ridge between the shoulders). Make sure the floor is level.

4 Each measurement must be taken three times to get an average. Capture video and photographic evidence of the entire process.

5 Submit your canine calculations online at **www. guinnessworldrecords.com/animals**.

6 Wait for the evidence to be assessed by our group of experts. If successful, you will receive an official GWR certificate for your high-reaching hound!

FAST FACT

To date, the record of **tallest dog** has only been held by one of two breeds: Great Danes and Irish wolfhounds. The holder prior to Freddy was Great Dane Zeus, who was the **tallest dog ever** (see pp.188–89).

The current holder of the record for **tallest female dog** is Lizzy, a Great Dane from Florida, USA, who stands 96.41 cm (3 ft 1.96 in) tall. Pictured here with her owner, Greg Sample, Lizzy is a black-and-white (or "harlequin") Great Dane, while her male counterpart Freddy has a mottled "merle" coat.

PIG WITH WINGS

For tired or stressed travellers at San Francisco International Airport, USA, relief comes in four-legged form. A dedicated "Wag Brigade" of animal "therapists" includes dogs, cats and rabbits. The newest member of this cheering team is a Juliana pig named LiLou (see p.201). Her painted trotters and various outfits – ballerina, nurse and, of course, pilot – ensure that she *hogs* the limelight and lifts the spirits of weary passengers!

ANIMALS AT WORK

HIGHEST-RANKING...

Attention! You're about to meet the record-breaking animals that have worked their way up the ranks to prestigious roles in a range of traditionally human professions.

NO WAY!

Sir Nils was made a knight in 2008!

PENGUIN

Sir Nils Olav started out as a Sergeant of the Norwegian Royal Guards in 1987. But on 22 Aug 2016, he was promoted to Brigadier. Here, Sir Nils – who is fittingly a *king* penguin – is inspecting his troops at Edinburgh Zoo in Scotland, UK, where he lives.

He hasn't done *baaaaad* for a sheep...

SHEEP

Promoted from the rank of Private on 1 Sep 2015, Lance Corporal Derby is the mascot of the Mercian Regiment. As a serving member of the British Armed Forces, the respectable ram is entitled to a salary, which covers his food and vet bills, and also days off.

CITY HALL

On 18 Nov 2014, rescue dog Frida the Chihuahua was officially made Mayor of San Francisco for a day to promote animal shelters. During her 24 hours in office, she was sworn in at City Hall (above) before visiting several local landmarks.

CAMEL

Meet Bert, probably the hairiest and definitely the humpiest member of the Los Angeles County Sheriff's Department in California, USA. His name stands for: **B**e **E**nthusiastic, **R**esponsible & **T**ruthful. Promoted to Reserve Sergeant in 2016, Bert is pictured here with his handler Nance Fite.

FAST FACT

Bert isn't the first of his kind to work in the field of law and order. His ancestors were military camels at Fort Tejon in California – a former US Army garrison in the mid-19th century.

SHERIFF

LOS ANGELES COUNTY SHERIFF

LEARNER GUIDE DOGS

By 31 Dec 2016, the UK's Guide Dogs for the Blind Association (aka Guide Dogs) had taught 33,910 graduates – the most guide dogs trained by an organization. In 2017, Guinness World Records was invited to one of the charity's canine academies to see the trainee assistance dogs in action.

Georgina Butcher has been a guide-dog trainer for seven years. As a veteran, she was the perfect person to show us around Guide Dogs' Redbridge school in London, UK. Pups spend their first year or so in a home setting with a "puppy walker", learning basic commands and social skills. They head to school for more advanced training aged 14–17 months.

GUINNESS WORLD RECORDS

CERTIFICATE

The most guide dogs trained by an organization is 33,910, achieved by The Guide Dogs for the Blind Association (UK) as of 31 December 2016

QUICK QUIZ

Q. WHICH IS THE MOST COMMON BREED AT GUIDE DOGS?

A. GOLDEN RETRIEVER CROSS

Learning in a school environment only gets a guide dog so far... During the later stages, trainers take to the streets to see how their pupils cope with all the temptations and distractions of the real world. One of the key skills every dog needs to perfect is crossing roads (below), a test that is carried out blindfolded – albeit under close supervision!

Training starts on quieter roads, then works up to busy high streets.

For safety reasons, trainers always work in pairs during blindfolded road tests like this.

The indoors presents a whole different set of challenges for people with sight loss. With this in mind, inside training focuses on obstacles such as opening doors (below left), passing through narrow gaps and walking up and down stairs (right). Many of the Guide Dogs trainers use clickers (above left), as well as doggie treats, as a means of positive reinforcement so the dogs know when they've done something right!

As Georgina comes to a doorway, Labrador Lacey knows that she must sit and wait patiently.

No time for play right now – I'm on duty!

For most dogs, it's hard to resist greeting a fellow hound or chasing a cat. But for guide dogs, that isn't an option while at work: running to another pet could seriously injure their owner. To prepare these assistance animals for inevitable encounters like this, the school has a group of "distraction dogs", such as this playful corgi, which are brought in by volunteers.

FUR-THER INFO

In the UK today, almost 2 million people are living with sight loss and, of those, around 180,000 rarely leave their homes alone. Since it was founded in 1934, the charity Guide Dogs has provided individual support that overcomes the challenges faced by people living with sight loss. To find out more about Guide Dogs and how you can get involved, visit **www.guidedogs.org.uk**.

GUIDE DOGS

As a guide dog becomes more experienced, the obstacle course is made increasingly more difficult!

Here, Georgina's colleague Charlotte Fowler walks Misty around the Guide Dogs obstacle course. This run of traffic cones, screens and other barriers helps to teach a number of important lessons. Firstly, it enables the young recruits to get used to wearing a harness – a key piece of kit that aids communication between human and dog.

The obstacles also build up a sense of spatial awareness. When out and about, a guide dog has to assess whether both itself and its owner can fit through a tight gap.

CAUTION Guide dog in training

THE EAGLE HUNTRESS

The Eagle Huntress poster — "A TRULY ENCHANTING, HEART WARMING AND UPLIFTING TALE." A FILM BY OTTO BELL

A teenage girl in the remote Altai Mountains of Mongolia has mastered an art traditionally practised by men: hunting with a golden eagle. A 2016 documentary told her story...

The Eagle Huntress premiered at the Sundance Film Festival in 2016. The BAFTA-nominated movie was directed by British film-maker Otto Bell and narrated by Daisy Ridley, who played Rey in *Star Wars Episode VII: The Force Awakens*.

FAST FACT

Kazakh hunters use female eagles, which are larger and more fierce than males. They return the birds to the wild after seven years, when they've reached breeding maturity.

Profits made from the film have been put into an education fund for Aisholpan, who wants to be a doctor.

Aisholpan Nurgaiv is a Kazakh nomad from western Mongolia. There, near the borders with Russia, China and Kazakhstan, the men in her family have been hunting with golden eagles for at least 12 generations. The birds are trained to catch foxes and rabbits for fur and meat – a practice usually passed down from father to son. But when Aisholpan's elder brother, Samarkan, was drafted into the Mongolian army, she took his place and started hunting with her father. Three years later, film-makers arrived just in time to witness the then-13-year-old Aisholpan capture her own eaglet from a lofty mountain nest. She and the bird went on to win the area's annual falconry competition, beating all her male rivals.

PERFECT PARTNERS

In English, Aisholpan's name translates as "Moon Venus".

Aisholpan went to the USA and Canada for screenings of _The Eagle Huntress_. She was joined by her father Nurgaiv (aka Agalai) and her mother Almagul (aka Alma). Agalai is a veteran eagle hunter. It's a tough job; he has missing teeth from being thrown from his horse, and a scar from when an eagle talon pierced right through his hand!

Eagle hunters often have to ride one-handed. The other arm, thickly padded, acts as a perch for the bird. Strength is needed – a hunting golden eagle weighs about the same as a large bowling ball! Kazakh hunters also have to endure freezing conditions in winter, and occasionally go up into the mountains alone. Becoming a fully fledged eagle hunter usually takes five years of hard training – which makes Aisholpan's early success all the more impressive.

Mozambique tribesmen form working partnerships with wild greater honeyguides. The birds lead the way to beehives hidden in trees. The humans take the honey, while their avian assistants eat the wax.

Bottlenose dolphins in Laguna, Brazil, help local fishermen by driving mullet towards them. The dolphins then "signal", with head or tail slaps, for the nets to be thrown – and get to feed on any escaping fish.

Female pigs have traditionally been used to hunt for truffles because of their attraction to the fungi's smell. They can detect truffles as deep as 3 ft (0.9 m) underground!

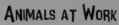

ANIMAL HELPERS

Sometimes our four-legged friends are more than just pets. Some are so clever and keen to help that they learn special skills to assist us in our day-to-day lives. Meet the caring animals that are always happy to lend a helping paw, hoof or even trotter!

ZOE

In 2013, miniature horse Zoe joined Zaiden Beattie at elementary school in Anchorage, Alaska, USA. Zaiden has a disorder that makes walking difficult, so having the pony close to hand helped to keep him steady. In addition to learning useful tasks such as picking things up that Zaiden couldn't reach, Zoe has also proved to be a loyal and affectionate companion.

A miniature horse stands no more than 96 cm (38 in) tall.

CUPCAKE

Long-haired Chihuahua Cupcake is the **smallest service dog**, standing a mere 15.8 cm (6.2 in) tall when measured on 8 Sep 2012. She may be tiny, but she is as solid as a rock to her doting owner, Angela Bain of New Jersey, USA. As well as having helped Angela through some traumatic experiences, Cupcake regularly makes visits to hospitals and charity events to cheer others.

NO WAY!
Zoe wears special sneakers indoors!

ARMSTRONG

Golden Labrador retriever Armstrong was the very **first diabetes-detection dog**. In 2003, he was trained to smell chemical changes in the human body that result in low blood-sugar levels. This can be very dangerous for diabetics, so raising the alarm early can mean the difference between life and death. Armstrong's success led to the founding of the charity Dogs4Diabetics in 2004.

Armstrong helped with pioneering research in California, USA.

ZEN

Perky Pomeranian Zen (right) is not just the best friend of American Eskimo dog Hoshi (left) – he's also his personal guide! The adorable pair from Washington, USA, bonded when Zen was rescued from the streets, several months before Hoshi lost his sight. Now, Zen seems to understand his bigger pal needs a helping paw.

PICKLES

Pickles from London, UK, is one super-smart cat. His owner, Kim Ward, has poor vision and has trained him to help find and fetch things, such as her cellphone or objects from upstairs.

But everyday items aren't the only thing this "guide cat" is able to detect... Kim also suffers from seizures and Pickles has somehow learned to perceive when they will happen and alert her. *Miaow*-vellous!

LILOU

At San Francisco International Airport in California, USA, "therapy" pig LiLou greets stressed-out travellers and amuses them with tricks. LiLou is part of the airport's groundbreaking "Wag Brigade", an animal team identified by jackets saying "Pet Me!" A fellow worker is Labrador retriever Marisol (below left), who loves nothing more than a tummy rub!

Who said that pigs can't fly?

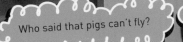

The Wag Brigade knows just how to relax nervous flyers.

DOGS on ICE

The Iditarod Trail Sled Dog Race covers a huge expanse of snowy wilderness in Alaska, USA. The 2017 edition of the event resulted in some breathtaking records – a tribute to both the dogs and their owners.

IDITAROD
National Historic Trail

Mile 0
Seward, Alaska

Sledding with dogs, aka mushing, is a passion with the Seavey family. On 14 Mar 2017, Mitch Seavey (left) achieved the **fastest time to complete the Iditarod Trail**. He reached the finish line in 8 days 3 hr 40 min 13 sec with his brilliant dog team, led by Pilot and Crisp (left). In doing so, Mitch notched up his third Iditarod win, and beat his son Dallas, the defending champion and four-time winner. Mitch also became the **oldest person to win the Trail**, at 57 years old. He summed up his victory in one word: "Sweet".

FAST FACT
The historic Iditarod Trail began as a transport route between Alaska's coast and the interior. Intrepid sled teams once delivered vital medicine to the town of Nome, stricken by an epidemic of diphtheria.

The Iditarod Trail has been operating since 1910. This makes it the **oldest sled-dog trail**. The race was set up in 1967 to save Alaskan huskies, which were being phased out in favour of snowmobiles.

Mitch arriving in Nome – the final Iditarod stop – on 14 Mar 2017.

GUINNESS WORLD RECORDS

I told them not to wash reds and whites together!

One of the rules of the race is that the huskies must wear special booties to protect their paws. The dogs, 16 to a team, also wear harnesses that capture as much of their energy as possible, and they may cosy up in warm jackets while resting.

Mushers often make their dogs' booties themselves.

The Iditarod race starts on the coast at Anchorage and ends at Nome, a former gold-mining town. Covering 1,049 mi (1,688 km), it's currently the **longest sled-dog race**. Mushers and animals brave frozen rivers, mountain ranges and Arctic tundra. Winds can be blinding and temperatures drop to −100°F (−73°C). *Brr!*

Rick Swenson is known as the "King of the Iditarod". He has achieved the **most wins of the Iditarod** – five – taking the title first in 1977 at 27 years old. He went on to win in 1979, 1981–82 and 1991 – on two occasions by less than five minutes. Rick is also the only musher to have won in three different decades.

QUICK QUIZ

Q. THE ALASKAN HUSKY IS THE FASTEST SLED DOG. WHAT SPEED CAN IT REACH?

A. 30 KM/H (19 MPH)

START

The huskies' schedule is carefully planned by their mushers. Some travel at night, some in the day, and each has their own feeding and resting routines. Proper fuelling and enough "zzz"s are essential – even for the hardiest hound!

ON ACTIVE DUTY

Armies all over the world rely on the superior strength and advanced senses of animals to win wars and save lives. Let's salute the brave beasts that went above and beyond the call of duty on the battlefield!

DANGER! MINES

GAMBIAN POUCHED RAT

The strong sense of smell of this African rodent has been put to good use. Pouched rats are trained to respond to the scent of an explosive by scratching the ground around it. Weighing less than 3 lb (1.3 kg), the rats are light enough not to trigger a detonation. They're the **smallest mammals to detect mines**. In 2003, a team of nine rats successfully identified 20 land mines in Mozambique.

LUCCA

Lucca the German shepherd is the 67th recipient of the Dickin Medal – the **highest award for animal gallantry**. Introduced in 1943 by Maria Dickin, founder of the People's Dispensary for Sick Animals (PDSA), the medal recognizes extreme courage or devotion to duty during a military conflict. This animal equivalent of the British Victoria Cross has so far been given to 32 messenger pigeons, 31 dogs (including Judy, see right), three horses and one cat.

Lucca, who lost a leg in 2012 while sniffing out a roadside bomb in Afghanistan, is the first US Marine Corps dog to receive the medal. She served for six years and is now enjoying her well-deserved retirement!

NO WAY!
Lucca served in over 400 missions!

Lucca travelled to London in 2016 to accept the medal with her owner, Gunnery Sgt Chris Willingham.

FAST FACT
On 2 Dec 1943, carrier pigeons Tyke, White Vision and Winkie became the **first animals to receive the Dickin Medal**. The messages they delivered led to the rescue of survivors from three plane crashes in WWII.

DOLPHINS & SEA LIONS

As of 2017, some 50 sea lions – such as Jack (above) – and 85 bottlenose dolphins (right) make up the **largest military division of marine mammals**. They're part of the US Navy Marine Mammal Program, based in San Diego, California, USA. Since 1960, it has trained sea creatures in duties that include removing underwater mines and detecting enemy divers.

Meet Lance Corporal Cruachan IV of the Royal Regiment of Scotland – a big title for a little horse! The Shetland pony is one of nine publicly funded official mascots currently employed by the British Armed Forces.

JUDY

During WWII, English pointer Judy endured sinking ships, jungle treks and several years in prisoner-of-war (PoW) camps. Captured in 1942 with the crew of HMS *Grasshopper*, she was the **first PoW dog** and helped to raise the spirits of her fellow human inmates. In 1946, she was awarded the Dickin Medal for gallantry (see left).

Fusilier Llywelyn is a Kashmiri goat in the First Battalion of the Royal Welsh. Along with regimental duties, he also takes part in UK parades, such as the Queen's 90th birthday celebrations in 2016.

MURPHY

Donkeys may be known for being stubborn, but as the **bravest donkey**, Murphy from Australia was all about cooperation. He was one of several beasts of burden who carried wounded soldiers to safety during WWI. In a ceremony held at the Australian War Memorial in 1997 (below), Murphy was belatedly awarded the RSPCA's Purple Cross for his great courage in the face of danger.

Here, the UK's Duchess of Cambridge meets the Irish Guards' official mascot: wolfhound Domhnall of Shantamon. Like all army mascots, he's entitled to a military rank, salary and rations – in his case, dog food!

Australian Army donkey Simpson accepted the medal on Murphy's behalf (Murphy is shown in the statue).

ANIMAL CAFÉS

There's a global craze for coffee with cuddles – cafés where customers come for the animal residents as much as for the cake. While being soothed by a serpent may not be everyone's cup of tea, there are plenty of establishments that specialize in cuter creature comforts...

A place for the *purr*fect cuppa? That's got to be a cat café! Japan has more than 300 of them, which means it can boast the **most cat cafés per country**. Tokyo alone has more than 60, including Temari no Ouchi (left). Many landlords in Japan don't allow people to keep pets. So, in the absence of a furry friend at home, animal-lovers seek out cafés where they can cuddle and play with a moggie. It's a great way to unwind if you're *feline* stressed after a hard day's work!

猫力フェ
.ka
ハピ猫
TEL03-3770-1328
道玄坂クラトスビル3F

CAT

FAST FACT

Cat cafés originated in Chinese Taipei, where the first one – Cat Flower Garden – opened in the late 1990s. Japanese visitors took the concept back to their own country, where the first cat café to open was in Osaka in 2004.

For those in Japan who like their drinks well chilled, the Penguin Izakaya Ryote in Tokyo (above) would be a n-*ice* place to go. But it's not the only venue with black-and-white, flippered residents. The **first penguin café** was Penguin Bar Fairy, which opened in Matsuyama on the Japanese island of Okinawa in 2008.

Le Café des Chats in Montreal, Canada, opened its doors in 2014, and is the first permanent cat café in North America. It borrowed the idea of cat cafés from Asia, but its main purpose is to find new homes for stray or unwanted kitties. The café works closely with local animal shelters, and customers popping in for refreshments sometimes find themselves taking home a furry friend...

The Owl Café in Tokyo, Japan, is so popular that you have to book! Customers can spend an hour with one of the 20 or so hand-reared birds perched around the room. Sounds like a hoot!

You can get a boa with your cola at Japan's Tokyo Snake Center, which opened in 2015. It displays around 35 snakes of 20 different species, including a ball python, a San Francisco garter and a Baron's green racer. Daring diners can pay a bit extra to handle the serpents. Anyone for a Honduran milk snake? (Warning: it's *not* a drink!)

A corn snake keeps one table company. Each box is labelled with the snake's name, gender and species.

NO WAY!
A hedgehog can have up to 8,000 spines!

Hedgehogs are not so hard to handle – as a café in Tokyo sets out to show. The venue's name, Harry, is a play on the Japanese word for hedgehog, *harinezumi*, which literally means "needle mouse". Visitors don't seem too worried about the prickles, queuing up to spend an hour with these spiny little bundles of joy.

While hedgehogs have prickly backs, they can still be handled with care.

SPORTS STARS

There's nothing like a real animal mascot to delight the fans – and in some cases intimidate the opposition. From burly bison to crowing cockerels, these dedicated team players are always guaranteed to drive the crowd *wild*!

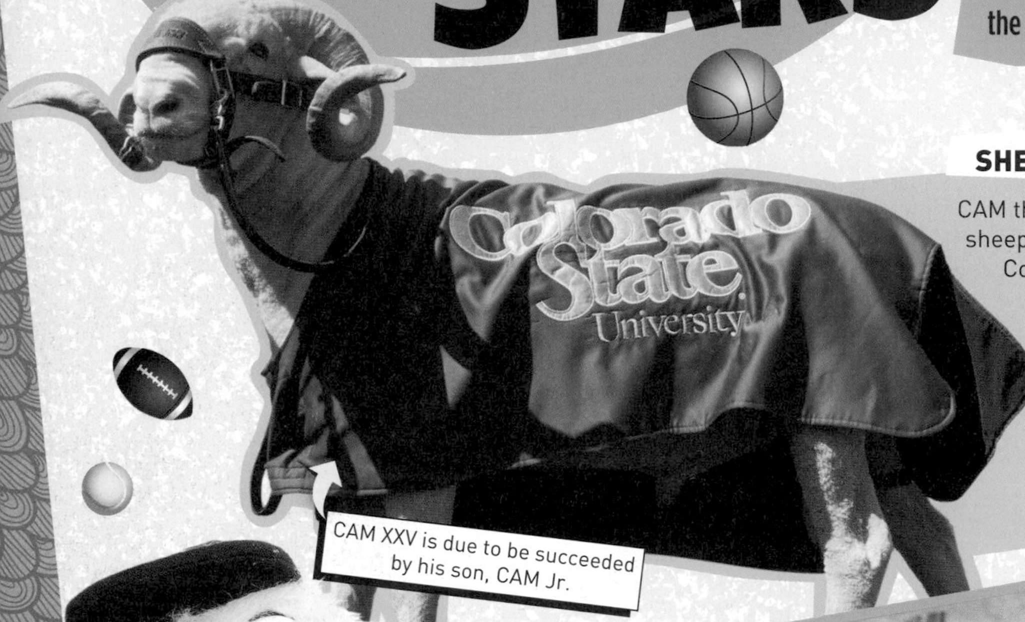

SHEEP

CAM the Ram is a Rambouillet sheep, a breed that has fronted Colorado State University athletics teams since 1945. The current CAM is the 25th to hold the job. He is the focal point of home games, cheering on his team with his student "Ram Handlers".

CAM XXV is due to be succeeded by his son, CAM Jr.

SIR BIG SPUR
THE MOST INVOLVED MASCOT IN SPORTS

GO COCKS

SIR BIG SPUR'S ROOST

COCKEREL

The University of South Carolina's sports teams are known as the "Gamecocks". So, fittingly, their football mascot is a red-and-black cockerel: Sir Big Spur IV. His roost is the best seat in the arena!

On 13 Sep 2016, the Chicago White Sox baseball team brought together the **most dogs at a sporting event**: 1,122. The Sox were cheered on to win against the Cleveland Indians at their home stadium. One of the canine fans is pictured here with the Sox's green mascot, Southpaw.

BISON

The Colorado Buffaloes' mascot – Ralphie – charges around the university stadium in Boulder, Colorado, USA. Guided by varsity athletes, the American football team's animal star is always a female bison, as they're slightly easier to control than males.

SHETLAND PONY

The SMU Mustangs represent Southern Methodist University in Dallas, Texas, USA. The American football team's mascot since 1932 has been a black Shetland pony named Peruna. During games, the pony – currently Peruna IX – trots triumphantly across the field whenever his team scores!

BULLDOG

Each successive mascot for the University of Georgia Bulldogs is called Uga – an abbreviation of the uni's full name. For more than 60 years, they have come from one family of English bulldogs. Uga's predecessors even have their own mausoleum at the stadium!

Uga has his own custom-built, air-conditioned dog house at the stadium!

Keep your eyes on the prize, boys...

GOLDEN EAGLE

German soccer team Eintracht Frankfurt have majestic golden eagle Attila as their lucky charm. In one 2016 match, striker Haris Seferovic borrowed one of Attila's feathers and kept it in his sock during a game. Result? A win, of course.

QUIZ ANSWERS

P.13: HYBRID ANIMAL QUIZ

1. Shoat/geep

2. Wholphin

3. Grolar/pizzly

PP.50–51: CAMOUFLAGE

1. *Two* **screech owls**

2. Geometer moth larva masquerading as bird poo!

3. Stonefish

4. Pygmy seahorse

5. Malayan jungle nymph

6. Titan stick insect

7. Snow leopard

1. William & Kate
Hamster

2. Cara Delevingne
Rabbit

3. Ed Sheeran
Cats

4. Miley Cyrus
Dogs
Pig
Cats

5. DanTDM
Pugs

6. Reese Witherspoon
Miniature donkeys

ANIMAL CHARITIES DIRECTORY

AMERICAN★HUMANE
FIRST TO SERVE™
American Humane
Washington, DC, USA
Founded: 1877
www.americanhumane.org
800-227-4645

Battersea Dogs & Cats Home
London, UK
Founded: 1860
www.battersea.org.uk
0843 509 4444

BLUE CROSS OF INDIA · MADRAS
Blue Cross of India
Chennai, India
Founded: 1964
bluecrossofindia.org
044-22300666

GUIDE DOGS
Guide Dogs
Reading, UK
Founded: 1934
www.guidedogs.org.uk
0118 983 5555

SPCA 愛護動物協會
Hong Kong SPCA
Hong Kong, China
Founded: 1903
www.spca.org.hk
852-2802-0501

mayhew
for dogs, cats and communities
The Mayhew Animal Home
London, UK
Founded: 1886
www.themayhew.org
020 8962 8000

MORRIS ANIMAL REFUGE
- America's First Animal Shelter -
Morris Animal Refuge
Philadelphia, Pennsylvania, USA
Founded: 1874
www.morrisanimalrefuge.org
215-735-9570

PAWS · 1954 · THE PHILIPPINE ANIMAL WELFARE SOCIETY
The Philippine Animal Welfare Society
Quezon City, Philippines
Founded: 1954
www.paws.org.ph
632-475-1688

THE WILD ANIMAL SANCTUARY
The Wild Animal Sanctuary
Keenesburg, Colorado, USA
Founded: 1980
www.wildanimalsanctuary.org
303-536-0118

INDEX

PICTURE CREDITS

1 Kevin Scott Ramos/GWR; **3** Kevin Scott Ramos/GWR; **4** Paul Michael Hughes/GWR, Alamy, Reuters, Melissa Gayle; **5** Kevin Scott Ramos/GWR, Alamy, Ryan Schude/GWR; **7** Paul Michael Hughes/GWR; **8** iStock; **10** Shutterstock, Alamy; **11** Shutterstock, Alamy; **12** Shutterstock, Jamers Ellerker/GWR, Splash; **13** Alamy, James Ellerker/GWR, Shutterstock, Reuters; **14** Reuters, Getty; **15** Reuters, Alamy; **16** Shutterstock, Alamy; **17** Shutterstock, Alamy; **18** Alamy; **19** Alamy, Shutterstock; **20** Alamy; **21** Wyss Institute at Harvard University, BBC; **22** Reuters; **23** Reuters, Alamy, iStock, Getty; **24** Kevin Scott Ramos/GWR; **25** Taylor Herring/GWR, Ryan Schude/GWR; **26** Alamy; **28** Richard Bradbury/GWR, James Ellerker/GWR; **29** Richard Bradbury/GWR, Ryan Schude/GWR, Alamy, Kevin Scott Ramos/GWR; **30** James Ellerker/GWR, Richard Bradbury/GWR; **31** Alamy, Ryan Schude/GWR, Kevin Scott Ramos/GWR; **32** Shutterstock; **34** Paul Michael Hughes/GWR, Alamy, Getty; **35** Alamy, Arkive/Francesco Rovero; **36** Alamy, Shutterstock; **37** iStock, Alamy, Shutterstock; **38** Shutterstock, Alamy, Getty; **39** Shutterstock, Alamy, Nature PL; **40** Alamy, Jurgen Otto, Alamy; **41** Shutterstock, Getty, Alamy, iStock; **42** Getty, Alamy; **43** Ken Bohn/San Diego Zoo Global, Alamy, Shutterstock; **44** Alamy, iStock; **45** Alamy, FLPA; **46** Alamy; **47** Shutterstock, Alamy; **48** Alamy, Reuters; **49** Alamy; **50** iStock, Shutterstock; **51** Shutterstock, Ardea, FLPA, Ardea; **52** Alamy; **54** Kevin Scott Ramos/GWR; **56** James Ellerker/GWR; **57** Carley Garantziotis/GWR, Getty, Shutterstock; **58** Ryan Schude/GWR; **59** Reuters, PA; **60** Solent News, Alamy; **61** Alamy, Martin Le May, Shutterstock; **62** Paul Michael Hughes/GWR; **63** Alamy; **64** Alamy; **65** Getty, Caters; **66** Shutterstock; **70** Alamy; **71** Getty, Ronald Grant Archive, Alamy; **72** Shutterstock, Alamy, Imagenet; **73** Alamy, Imagenet; **74** Alamy, Matt Groening; **75** Getty, Alamy, Getty; **76** Shutterstock, Alamy; **77** Games Press, Alamy, Games Press, Moby; **78** Facebook; **79** Ken Bohn/San Diego Zoo, Alamy; **80** YouTube; **81** YouTube; **82** Instagram; **84** Kevin Scott Ramos/GWR, Getty; **85** Getty; **86** EmojiOne, Shutterstock; **87** Shutterstock; **88** Caters; **90** Ronald Mackechnie/GWR; **91** Getty, AP, Caters, Tamara Reynolds;

92 Getty, Alamy, SWNS; **93** RSPCA, WA Police, Shutterstock; **96** Caters; **97** Caters; **98** Getty, Shutterstock, Alamy; **99** Alamy, Getty, Caters; **100** Shutterstock; **101** Alamy; **102** Alamy; **103** AP, Reuters, Alamy, Getty; **105** Fox, Getty, Tripp Yeoman; **106** James Cannon/GWR; **107** James Cannon/GWR, Simon Wilkinson; **108** Paul Michael Hughes/GWR; **110** Jonathan Browning/GWR, Shinsuke Kamioka/GWR, Shinsuke Kamioka/GWR; **111** Paul Michael Hughes/GWR; **112** Paul Michael Hughes/GWR; **113** Carley Garantziotis/GWR, Shutterstock; **114** Paul Michael Hughes/GWR; **115** James Ellerker/GWR, Paul Michael Hughes/GWR, Getty, Alamy; **116** Paul Michael Hughes/GWR; **117** Alamy; **118** Getty; **119** Getty, Shutterstock; **120** Caters, Getty; **121** Caters, AP, Alamy; **122** Melissa Gayle; **123** James Ellerker/GWR; **124** Ryan Schude/GWR; **126** Tripp Yeoman; **127** Tripp Yeoman; **128** Tripp Yeoman; **129** Tripp Yeoman; **130** Tripp Yeoman; **131** Tripp Yeoman; **132** Barb D'Arpino; **134** Alamy; **135** Alamy, Getty; **136** Alamy; **137** Getty; **139** Shutterstock; **140** Reuters, Alamy, Shutterstock; **141** Shutterstock, Getty, Alamy; **142** Reuters, Alamy; **143** Getty, Alamy, Shutterstock; **144** Paul Michael Hughes/GWR, Shutterstock, Reuters; **145** Reuters; **146** Angela Bohlke, Charles Kinsey, Artyom Krivosheev; **147** Alison Mees, Adam Parsons, Edward Kopeschny, Anup Deodhar; **148** David Slater; **149** Vadim Trunov/Solent News, Caters, Shutterstock; **150** Shutterstock; **152** Alamy; **153** Alamy; **154** Shutterstock, Kevin Scott Ramos/GWR; **155** Getty, Alamy; **156** Alamy, Shutterstock; **157** Alexander Kabanov, Alamy; **158** Reuters, Alamy; **159** Reuters; **160** Alamy, The Gorilla Foundation; **161** Shutterstock, Alamy; **162** Chester Zoo, Taronga Zoo, La Palmyre Zoo; **163** Theo Kruse/Royal Burgers' Zoo, Taronga Zoo, Jonas Verhulst/ZOO Antwerpen, Chester Zoo; **164** Al Diaz/GWR; **165** Shutterstock, Getty; **166** Alamy; **167** Alamy, Shutterstock; **168** Alamy;

169 Alamy; **171** Shutterstock; **174** Paul Michael Hughes/GWR; **176** Kevin Scott Ramos/GWR, Shutterstock; **178** Shutterstock, Reuters; **179** Caters, Reuters, Shutterstock; **180** Getty; **181** Alamy, Shutterstock, SWNS; **182** The Guardian, Caters; **183** Alamy, Caters; **184** Richard Bradbury/GWR; **185** Shutterstock; **186** Shutterstock, Alamy, James Ellerker/GWR; **187** Richard Bradbury/GWR, James Ellerker/GWR; **188** Shutterstock, Alamy, Kevin Scott Ramos/GWR; **189** Ryan Schude/GWR, Shutterstock, Kevin Scott Ramos/GWR; **190** Paul Michael Hughes/GWR; **191** Shutterstock, Al Diaz/GWR; **194** Shutterstock; **195** Corporal Andy Reddy RLC, Reuters, Ranald Mackechnie/GWR; **196** James Cannon/GWR; **197** James Cannon/GWR; **198** Alamy, Imagenet; **199** Shutterstock, Alamy, Claire Spottiswoode, Getty; **200** Shutterstock, Philip Robertson/GWR; **201** Dogs4Diabetics, SWNS; **202** SuperStock, Jeff Schultz, David Dodman, KNOM Radio Mission; **203** Alamy, SuperStock; **204** Alamy, Shutterstock; **205** Shutterstock, Alamy, Getty, Crown Copyright; **206** Alamy, Shutterstock; **207** Getty, PA, Reuters; **208** Shutterstock, David Durochik, Getty; **209** Alamy, Shutterstock, Getty; **210** Shutterstock, IStock, Alamy, Ardea, FLPA; **211** Alamy

ACKNOWLEDGEMENTS

Lally Baker (Fitzpatrick Referrals Ltd), Rosie Barclay (Association of Pet Behaviour Councillors, www.apbc.org.uk), Andrew Bleiman (ZooBorns), Amanda Blenkhorn (Ripley's Aquariums), Tina Campanella (ZSL London), The Comedy Wildlife Photography Awards, Pat Craig (The Wild Animal Sanctuary), Chris Eastland (ZooBorns), Dr Sarah Ellis (International Cat Care, www.icatcare.org), James Fallin (SPAWAR), Professor Noel Fitzpatrick, Bec George (Battersea Dogs & Cats Home), Jennefer Maclean (Tolga Bat Rescue and Research), Bruce Nash (The-Numbers.com), Origami Way (www.origamiway.com), Dr Karl P N Shuker, Matthew White, Annabel Williams (Guide Dogs), Zoo Berlin

THE
GUINNESS WORLD RECORDS
COLLECTION

GUINNESS WORLD RECORDS 2018

GUINNESS WORLD RECORDS

GUINNESS
WORLD
RECORDS
2018

MEET OUR
REAL-LIFE
SUPERHEROES

THOUSANDS OF AMAZING NEW RECORDS!

GUINNESS WORLD RECORDS
VOLUME 11

intro by DanTDM

GAMER'S EDITION
THE ULTIMATE GUIDE TO GAMING RECORDS

SPECIAL SUPERHERO SECTION!

OUT NOW!

GUINNESS WORLD RECORDS
FOOTBALL EDITION

GUINNESS WORLD RECORDS
Science And Stuff
THE GROSSEST, SMELLIEST, NOISIEST & WEIRDEST

COMING SOON IN 2018!

GUINNESS WORLD RECORDS

WWW.GUINNESSWORLDRECORDS.COM/2018

Subject to region.